RÎMARU

BUTCHER OF BUCHAREST

by
Mike Phillips and Stejărel Olaru

Edited by Ramona Mitrică

27/05/201

PROFUSION CRIME SERIES

Profusion, London 2012

PROFUSION CRIME SERIES
Fiction / Non-Fiction

George Arion - *Attack in the Library*
Bogdan Hrib - *Kill the General*
Oana Stoica-Mujea - *Anatomical Clues*
Mike Phillips & Stejarel Olaru - *Rimaru, Butcher of Bucharest*
Series Editor: Mike Phillips

Published by Profusion International Creative Consultancy
mail@profusion.org.uk • www.profusion.org.uk

Rimaru - Butcher of Bucharest by Mike Phillips and Stejărel Olaru

Translations of Romanian archive documents by Ramona Mitrică and
Mihai Rîșnoveanu
Typesetting by SGS Creative

ISBN-13: 978-0956867636

RÎMARU

BUTCHER OF BUCHAREST

Part 1

Prologue

The spring and early summer of 1970 was an eventful and momentous period for Romania. April and May saw a combination of unusual and extreme weather conditions. Torrential rains were accompanied by high winds and a heatwave which melted the frozen icefields of the Carpathian mountaintops. In the first weeks of May, the rivers rising in the Carpathians or flowing down from the high ground into the Danube began to overflow, signalling the start of a notable disaster.

The Danube rises in Germany's Black Forest and runs through Austria and Hungary down to its Delta in South East Romania. Famed for its beauty and benevolence, the Danube has also been, by tradition, the most important transport and communications link between and within the regions it serves. As it nears its final destination, the river is fed by a multitude of streams rushing downhill from the Carpathians to join it, and these waters nourish the most heavily populated and intensely cultivated plains and valleys in the region. Within this landscape, floods are not unusual. 1970, however, was exceptional. In one hectic month, between the 12th of May and the middle of June, the floods killed more than two hundred people, drowned over a hundred thousand cattle and farm animals, and destroyed thousands of houses, leaving a quarter of a million people homeless. Low-lying villages were evacuated to centres higher up, the majority of farmland was inundated and industry went into recession.

After a fortnight, the waters had begun to recede, but another bout of rain and snow restarted the cycle, and it was another three weeks before the floods finally began to retreat.

The event was cataclysmic for a countryside still struggling to come to terms with the massive disruptions unleashed in previous decades by various official policies. The impact was even more troubling for a nation in the grip of various anxieties about its political future and identity.

In March 1965, Nicolae Ceaușescu, the new General Secretary of the Romanian Communist Party, had declared its independence from the diktats of the Kremlin, and reinforced the message later on in 1968 by refusing to join his Warsaw Pact neighbours in suppressing the Czech revolt. As the floods progressed, international aid and relief agencies began pouring in to assist the regime, now seen in the West as an Iron Curtain maverick. Ceaușescu himself, after a brief visit to Moscow, toured the affected areas, and made a point of being seen directing operations in Brăila and Galați, significant areas because of their heavy industry, storage facilities and proximity to the Danube ports. The nation had also been mobilised to meet the emergency. Public health officials and volunteers toured the country warning about the dangers of drinking untreated water, and inoculating the citizenry against typhoid. The military, reinforced by an army of construction workers and engineers, worked tirelessly to repair and replace dikes and flood defences. In this atmosphere, Ceaușescu seized every opportunity to take advantage of the mood of solidarity to reiterate his message of independence from Moscow, and to proclaim the unique status of the national identity.

In later years, Romanians would look back on this period as part of the regime's 'good years'. On the other hand, it was this same moment, the time of the floods, which unleashed the most dangerous and unrelenting predator the nation had ever seen.

****

The 15 most serious crimes of which Rîmaru was convicted.

8/9 May 1970 – Elena Oprea – premeditated murder

1/2 June 1970 – Florica Marcu – rape, mutilation and cannibalism

19/20 July 1970 – OCL Confecția store – theft of public property

24 July 1970 – Margareta Hanganu – assault, wounding and aggravated theft

22/23 November 1970 – Olga Bărăitaru – attempted murder, rape and aggravated theft

15/16 February 1971 – Gheorghița Sfetcu – attempted murder and aggravated theft

17/18 February 1971 – Elisabeta Florea – assault and attempted murder

4/5 March 1971 – Fănica Ilie – premeditated murder, rape and aggravated theft

8/9 April 1971 – Gheorghița Popa – murder, rape, cannibalism and aggravated theft

1/2 May 1971 – Stana Sărăcin – assault, wounding and attempted rape

4/5 May 1971 – Mihaela Ursu – murder, rape

4/5 May 1971 – Maria Iordache – assault and attempted murder

6/7 May 1971 – Margareta Enache – assault and attempted murder

6/7 May 1971 – Elena Buluci – assault and attempted murder

7 May 1971 – Iuliana Frunzinschi – assault, aggravated theft of public property and aggravated theft of private property

****

The Rîmaru family had its origins in Wallachia, the Principality which united with Moldavia during the 19th century to create modern day Romania. More precisely, the family sprang from Lesser Wallachia, now known as Oltenia, a patch of land lying between the Danube, the Southern Carpathians and the Olt River.

Oltenia shared the chequered history of its larger twin, Greater Wallachia (Muntenia), with a few special wrinkles of its own. The region came into existence as part of the First Bulgarian Empire, and after the 10th century, Hungary and Bulgaria jostled for a couple of hundred years over dominance of the territory. From the 15th century, however, the Ottoman Empire took control, a situation which persisted, only interrupted by brief periods of Russian occupation, until the unification of 1859 brought the Kingdom of Romania into existence.

Oltenia's history, however, had its own special flavour. Shaped by the politics of hundreds of years of anti-Ottoman struggle, the region threw up some of the figures who continue to dominate the imagination of Romanians. For example, Vlad the Impaler, the 15th century ruler and inspiration for the 19th century legend of Dracula, was famous for the bloodthirstiness of his reign and his campaigns against the Ottomans. He flourished in Northern Oltenia and gives us the first link between a ruler and the establishment of Bucharest as the administrative centre of the district.

By the first decades of the 20th century, the region could display a distinct pattern of leaders who were radical, ruthless and unfailingly violent. By tradition these figures had certain characteristics which were valued and endlessly celebrated in their environment. They were violent. They were self willed and rebellious, almost by reflex. The only authority they would accept had to be validated by the force of their own instincts, and they had the rare talent of being able to escape punishment or penalties for their murders and thefts.

A typical historical figure who became an Oltenian folk hero was the 19th century hajduk (bandit) Iancu Jianu, who was born into a family of boyars (hereditary aristocrats) in Caracal, which was also, later on, the same small town where Ion Rîmaru's parents, Florea and Ecaterina, grew up.

Jianu owned land and slaves, but he was vociferous about his opposition to the Ottoman policy of appointing Greek (Phanariot) rulers in preference to the local boyars. Returning home one day to find that he was being taxed, he killed the tax collector and ran away to assemble a band of outlaws which proceeded to rob and murder people all over

Wallachia. He was caught and imprisoned in 1812, but, after his relatives intervened, he was released. He returned to his life of brigandage and continued even after being pardoned. Finally, in 1817, he was again caught and sentenced to death by hanging, but he was saved by an old custom by which a condemned man could be reprieved if a woman proposes to marry him and he accepts. Safely married, Jianu settled down and lived comfortably for another three decades, even serving for a time as local official.

Another native of Caracal, closer to contemporary times, was Gheorghe Argeşanu, who was appointed Prime Minister by King Carol II in 1938, after the assassination of his predecessor Armand Călinescu by the fascist party, the Iron Guard. Among his first actions were the public display of the assassins' bodies, and the arrest and execution (without trial) of three Iron Guard members – in each county. Later on, after the Iron Guard took over the Romanian government, Argeşanu was killed as part of the massacre at Jilava prison when over 60 political prisoners were murdered in one night.

All this was part of an active living memory in Caracal.

****

Ask the average Romanian about Caracal and their first reaction will be surprise that a foreigner has even heard of the place. The next reaction will be, more or less, derogatory. "Caracal?" "It's nowhere." "A hole." "The most depressing place I've ever been in." And so on.

Romanians, therefore, seem to talk about Caracal in much the same way as Americans mention hillbilly and redneck territory. There is even an archaic witticism that exploits the Romanian love of wordplay, which turns on the meaning of *căruță cu proști*, an expression signifying a carriage/cart conveying fools or idiots. Where did the *căruță cu proști* crash/unload its passengers, the joke runs – answer, Caracal!

In contemporary times, Caracal is notable for being the town where the local authority built a proud new development, but then found that the contractors had forgotten to remove all their equipment, so that the walls of the new block of housing also enclosed an enormous crane.

It goes without saying that comments and stories of this kind do an injustice to Caracal. By the end of the 19th century, Caracal was the region's second most important city, at the centre of one of the most important agricultural districts in the country. The town had a moderately stable population, upwards of 30,000, and a notable role in the collection, storage and transportation of Oltenia's agricultural products. In this sense, it was an accurate reflection of Oltenia's status.

On the other side of the equation, the Oltenian population suffered a significant degree of fragmentation and pressure as a result of their own prominence in the politics and economy of the surrounding regions. Take the issue of agriculture. Oltenia was famous for its production of grain, a crop which imposed different demands to those coming from small scale peasant holdings. Until the latter part of the 19th century grain allowed for large scale landownership by boyar families, and, for a workforce composed of Roma slaves, corvée labour[1], and the rural poor.

---

1 A feudal hangover in which workers were attached to large estates and largely unpaid.

This was very far from a smiling landscape inhabited by a stable peasantry. Instead, most of the population were landless peasants, labourers plagued by a parasitic class of bandits (hajduks), and dependent on the whims of great landowners or boyar families. On top of all this, the entire population, both the privileged and the disenfranchised, were mere units in an economic and political structure shaped and controlled by foreign powers.

The Wallachian revolution of 1848 was an attempt to resolve some of these issues by wrestling local autonomy from the Russian administration, whose rule had been licensed by the Ottomans. It was led by a group of young officers, heavily influenced by the Romantic and Liberal trends driving revolutions all over Europe in that year. Under Russian pressure, the Ottomans suppressed the revolt, but, in its aftermath, a passionate debate sprang up which led to significant changes in the politics of the region. This period saw the emancipation of Roma slaves and the abolition of the corvée system, while clear outlines of future land reform were drawn up and massively supported by the peasants. These plans, however, were delayed and quashed by the landlords, and land reform went on the back burner for another generation. 15 years later, redistribution began in earnest, but the amount of land allocated to the peasants was tiny and these holdings were then taxed and regulated to such an extent that most of their owners were driven back into destitution. Another 50 years of intensifying poverty climaxed in the Peasants Revolt of 1907, which started in Moldavia but rapidly spread to Oltenia, and threatened, for a time, to set off a full blown revolution. Contemporary estimates suggest that about 3,000 people were killed during the army's ruthless crushing of the rebellion. Later on, eyewitnesses claimed that the regime's historians were exaggerating the figures, but there is no doubt that the peasants' revolt was a desperate response to desperate conditions.

By now, everyone of any importance knew about the peasants' disaffection and its causes, yet it was another 15 years before there was another attempt at land reform. Once again, however, the reforms did little to ameliorate the grinding poverty of the countryside. By the outset of World War Two, agriculture accounted for over 70% of Romania's national product, but half the arable land was owned by 8% of the landowners.

****

Little is known about Florea Rîmaru's early life before he was recruited into the army, but the fact that he joined as a common soldier and served throughout the conflict is a significant indication of his position in the society and his prospects. Given the history and the infrastructure of the region, the sons of the landless rural population in Oltenia were living on borrowed time.

Anyone who could arrange it escaped, joining the growing urban centres like Bucharest, or moving further afield. The great Romanian sculptor Brâncuşi left the life of an infant sheepherder to work in Craiova, the major city of the region, then moved to Bucharest, and from there to Munich, before travelling to Paris. Later on, the future dictator, Nicolae Ceauşescu, born in rural Oltenia around the same time as Florea Rîmaru, arrived in Bucharest at the age of 11, to follow his destiny.[2]

Florea Rîmaru was one of those who remained, part of the population pool available for recruitment, and the most notable fact about his army service was that he survived World War Two. The army he joined started its war on the Eastern Front, fighting with the Axis Powers against the Russians. It is estimated that a quarter of a million Romanian soldiers died in that campaign. Later on, the fascist Iron Guard government used elements of the army to pursue some of the most vicious aspects of the Nazis' anti-Semitic policies. When King Michael took Romania into the Allied camp, the army was committed to fighting their former allies in the German and Hungarian forces, driving through Moldavia and Wallachia down into Oltenia and across the Danube. The battle of Turda saw an entire month of the bloodiest fighting of the campaign. Survival was a lottery.

After the war, Florea married Ecaterina and they lived in Caracal, but there was nothing about their personal histories or environment which would have guaranteed a happy, settled existence. Florea drank, and, according to some reports, beat his wife daily. He had no skills and owned nothing. There was nothing to hold the couple in Caracal, and the next stop was Corabia, a small Danube port facing Bulgaria across the river.

Under the postwar Communist regime, Corabia was

---

2 One of the boyars who was most prominent in arguing the peasants' case for land reform in the wake of the 1848 revolution was named Ceauşescu. It is not clear whether the dictator was related to him, but it is an ironical footnote to the career of a politician who was an avid supporter of the expropriation involved in the collectivisation of agricultural resources.

about to diversify out of its role as a trans-shipment area into becoming a busy industrial centre with such enterprises as a sugar mill and a furniture manufacturing plant. There was work in Corabia, but, if Caracal was 'nowhere', Corabia was a sort of post restante to nowhere. After the excitements and traumas of the war, Florea was bored, depressed and angry, his state of mind complicated by the fact that he was convinced he had syphilis (lues), and, by his own account, he was debilitated by the illness in the two years before his son, Ion, was born in Corabia, on the 12th of October 1946.

****

On the surface, Corabia can boast some impressive features - an Orthodox cathedral, a remarkable Roman ruin (Castrum Sucidava), and a monument to the town's role in the Romanian War of Independence, while the riverside walks offer a succession of stunning views over the Danube.

In 1946, however, Corabia was a small port and border crossing, ravaged by war, whose inhabitants numbered less than 20,000. The river offered an easy passage in and out of the town, so individuals came and went at an even faster rate than the rest of the county, leaving behind a fragmented and unstable population, largely dependent on their role in the business of storage and trans-shipment. In the circumstances, the town had little to offer a young man like Florea, except drink, casual labour, and a series of unwelcome responsibilities.

The Rîmarus lived in 109 Timiş Street, a house belonging to Ecaterina's parents, Florea and Maria Ciocan. Timiş

Street was a side street of small and largely dilapidated properties, which ran across the main boulevards, at some distance from the pleasant views of the river, and on the other side of the town centre. There were two more children, Cornel, who was a boy nine years younger than Ion, and Georgeta Maria, five years younger.

Ion's health was delicate from early on. At the age of six he was treated for pneumonia, and when he turned sixteen he was committed to hospital with hepatitis. Then when he was eighteen he contracted gastritis which became aggravated while he was undergoing military training in a unit of pontoons at Turnu Măgurele. About two months after joining the army he was diagnosed during a medical inspection and sent to the hospital in Ploieşti where he spent two months being treated for a duodenal ulcer.

Apart from all this, Ion Rîmaru, by all accounts, had a difficult and troubled childhood. These reports, however, were gathered in the wake of Rîmaru's arrest and trial, as an official part of the subsequent investigation. It is not hard to imagine the response of the average citizen in that time, when asked about the childhood of a notorious killer by a member of the Militia or Securitate forces. Few people were likely to reply that Ion was a charming little chap with a sunny disposition. Corabia, in addition, was a tiny place, which, like the rest of the country, was going through a ferment of change, without the big city safety valves of anonymity and indifference.

The new postwar regime had, early on, identified children, especially the children of the previously oppressed proletariat, as an essential element in demonstrating the benefits of socialist equality. It was these children, mostly from a 'healthy' (proletarian) background, who would become 'new' men and women, and inherit the new world. Children, therefore, were an essential backdrop to every parade, and every display of civic identity, marching, singing, and waving flags. It was children who inhabited the healthy activities of the Pioneers[3] and exemplified the disciplined virtues of socialist education. Out of all the conceivable moments in history, this time and place must have been among the least accommodating in which a surly and rebellious teenager could find himself.

On the other hand, there is no doubt that Ion Rîmaru showed signs of having real and consistent problems. He was punished repeatedly at school, mostly for his inability to accomplish and complete his work. According to his parents, the teachers spoke to them repeatedly about his failure to apply himself. Until the 9th grade, at around the age of fourteen, he progressed from grade to grade at the bottom of the class, with no record of achievement except for the dislike and suspicion he attracted. Typically, he was given to violent outbursts of anger, he was known to torment and kill small animals, and he responded to his mother's admonishments with a brutal rudeness, echoing the brutal manners of his father, who, at a time when wife beating was not uncommon, shocked the neighbours by his treatment of his wife.

Ion was certainly suffering psychologically; and it is more than likely that he was also suffering physically from the digestive problems which led to his being diagnosed with oesophageal spasm, in Bucharest, at the age of twenty one, an exceptional condition for someone less than fifty years

---

3 A youth movement, partly based on Boy Scout principles.

old; but, however unreliable the diagnosis may have been, it is clear, in hindsight, that Ion needed various kinds of attention which were lacking in his environment.

His troubles grew more serious as he grew older. He was forced to repeat the 9th grade, a humiliating experience for someone who was already firmly stuck in the role of an outsider. Puberty added another dimension. He developed a relationship with a younger schoolmate, and they were discovered one day in flagrante. Unfortunately for Ion, she was the pubescent and virgin daughter of a primary school teacher. What ensued was described as 'a public scandal'. The result? More punishment and a deeper sense of isolation. To make matters worse, the girl died later of septicaemia.

Unsurprisingly, he then gravitated towards a life of youthful delinquency. There is no exact record of his teenage misdemeanors, but he was arrested and convicted in 1964, during his last year at the Lyceum, for his part in the theft of some melons from a local State Enterprise, C.A.P. Voința. The charge was 'aggravated theft', because, when the gang was surprised by the watchman, it was Ion who attacked the man and beat him ferociously. As a result, he was sentenced to five months imprisonment, half of which he served in the penitentiary at Caracal.

In spite of all this, Ion's school records show that he consistently achieved a perfect grade for his conduct. There may be two main reasons for this extraordinary contradiction. Firstly, it is possible that he had already developed a capacity for vicious behaviour and fully understood the necessity for wearing a mask of virtue, in order to avoid discovery and punishment. The second possibility may be that Rîmaru's teachers took into account his 'healthy' proletarian background, and avoided any likely official complications for themselves and the school by ticking the good conduct box whenever his name came up. Given Ion's indifference or ineptitude at hiding his delinquencies, the second explanation seems rather more convincing. It also goes some way towards answering another difficult question. How was it that Rîmaru himself escaped any kind of official notice for as long as he did?

The solution may be that this was a kind of perfect storm in which the history of the region and his family, his neglected childhood, and his perceived instability, met with the ideology of a dogmatic regime, to nourish the insanity of his activities. It may be that if the state had been more accommodating towards the diagnosis and treatment of mental problems Ion's would have been identified and dealt with earlier. The ideology of the regime, however, simply did not allow for the idea that the perfect socialist state could be the incubator of mental illness. It may also be the case that, if Ion had not emerged from an impeccable proletarian background, his behaviour and his disability might have been challenged earlier, along with his almost total failure at school.

In any case, between leaving the Lyceum in Corabia, in 1964, and his arrival in Bucharest, in 1966, at the Nicolae Bălcescu Institute (renamed in 1985 The University of Agronomic Sciences and Veterinary Medicine), Rîmaru went through a number of experiences which might be described as traumatic. He graduated, and passed the baccalaureate. He served a prison sentence. He was conscripted and discharged from the army, and he spent another two months in hospital while they investigated whether or not he had an ulcer.

Afterwards, he took the exams for admission to the Nicolae Bălcescu Institute and scraped a pass, with a grade of 5.33 (out of 10), the lowest possible entry qualification.

In the meantime the family was disintegrating. They had returned to Caracal in 1953, but this was not a success, and by the end of the decade they were back in Corabia. Florea then claimed that he had caught his wife with a man, but he continued to live with her until late in the sixties. At this point he got a job at the ITB Floreasca Garage in Bucharest. Floreasca was one of the newer districts of the city, settled in the interwar years by skilled workers, and for the regime it was one of the areas where its support was strongest. For Florea there was a sense that he had arrived.

In 1966 Ion Rîmaru had also arrived. At last he was in the city where his obsessions could flourish, and his dreams could be realised.

Chapter 1

Bucharest 1970

The winter was long and hard. A biting wind scoured the broad avenues of the city centre, prompting old exiles to talk about the incessant gales which propelled the frosts of Siberia through the streets of Moscow. On some nights the temperature dropped perilously close to minus 30 degrees. Citizens, now beginning to be inured to shortages and blackouts, welcomed in the new decade, wrapped themselves in thick overcoats and queued with a minimum of complaint, unaware that they were on the verge of something worse than just another difficult phase.

By the beginning of March, it seemed as if the snow and ice had been impacting the pavements for much too long, but, in Bucharest, spring erupts with an unexpected and violent passion.

The ice dissipates and the dingy grey of the clouds retreats into a dull mist around the foothills of the mountains to the north, to be replaced in the sky by pale blue and gold. The trees lining the Boulevard of the Aviators or stubbling the innumerable scruffy pieces of wasteland behind the housing blocks, begin to glow green with the long suppressed energy of months; and the margins of pockmarked streets start to be dusted yellow by the ubiquitous little daisies of the central plains, interspersed with tiny carnations and pelargoniums. In between all these, bristle clumps of wayside rosebushes crowned with little points of brilliant crimson.

By the spring of 1970, Ion Rîmaru had already been a student at the Veterinary School for 4 years, and he was in the middle of his 5th year. He had been obliged to repeat the second year, and now he was in the process of repeating his third year. He was a poor student, but he had actually found himself, once again, at the point of an unstated conflict which determined his environment, but about which he could do nothing.

The Nicolae Bălcescu Institute was one of the central actors in the agricultural sector's response to the government's attempts to increase productivity. The admission of such a poor quality student as Rîmaru had been a symptom of the institution's struggle to maintain student numbers, and conform to a new system of values. At the same time, it was impossible to pretend that Ion met the required standards. "Shy and semi-literate, with a very poor vocabulary and an extremely narrow set of interests", was the way that one of his professors described him, but there was little or nothing the institution could do about improving his capacity or, even, about getting rid of him.

Ion's career began to be a reprise of his schooldays. He neglected his studies, and absented himself from most of his classes. He made no close friends, and his colleagues found his behaviour strange, unpredictable and sometimes frightening. In general he seemed isolated and alone. At the same time it is clear that he had a large extended family. On his father's side there were three brothers and a sister living in the countryside. Another sister lived in Corabia. In

Bucharest there were various cousins, including a namesake, Ion Rîmaru. On his mother's side there were numerous family members all living in Bucharest. On the other hand, Florea was on familiar terms with only one of them, his cousin Ion, and, although his sister lived in Corabia, he couldn't remember where.

Nevertheless Rîmaru seems to have a close relationship with both of his parents. Although they were now separated, his mother came to Bucharest twice every month to receive an allowance from Florea. On these occasions she would visit Ion. His brother and sister also made regular visits. At the same time his father seems to have been monitoring his progress quite closely, but Ion's behaviour was now following a familiar pattern.

"As far as I remember, my son lived in a student hall of residence situated on Splaiul Independenței. Studying in year 2, that is university year 1967-1968, my son did not pass the grade and repeated the year. After having asked about this at the secretariat, I asked him what his plans were and he said the university was difficult but that he would attend re-examination in the autumn. He failed re-examination as well. Thus, during university year 1968-1969 he repeated year 2, which he graduated with a mediocre qualification.

During this year my son had obtained accommodation and meals, moving to Mărăști Boulevard in the halls of residence within the Nicolae Bălcescu Institute. In a discussion with the faculty secretary, she told me that my son was behaving badly towards people around him, he was dour and that it was because of this that he lost his scholarship.

In year 3, namely 1969-1970, he failed the grade again. I don't know what he did to repeat the year. I paid monthly the sum of 460 Lei for my son's canteen and residence, and I was striving to give my son a sum of pocket money monthly for his expenses, around 150 Lei. Besides this, my mother in law was also sending 50 or 100 Lei from time to time.

In the discussion with the faculty secretary at veterinary medicine, she informed me about my son's bad behaviour, that he was not learning, that when he was questioned by professors he stood up and did not reply. She also said that, because she saw him very tired, she suspected he was working somewhere at nights, as a waiter, or that he had a woman with whom he was living. In addition, Professor Bica told me to my face, in the presence of my son, that he did not learn, that he was unruly and that he had bad behaviour."

(28th of May 1971, Militia file 751/B/1971, vol. 1)

Rîmaru's classmates had a different impression of him. Florea Fulga was a schoolmate of Rîmaru's from Corabia. He was admitted to the Institute in 1968.

"Regarding Rîmaru Ion[4], I can say he had a closed personality during Lyceum, he was always reserved, and wouldn't converse with anybody. He treated me the same, even if for one trimester I stayed in the

4 In official documents - such as Militia records - Romanian names were listed according to the formula - family name followed by the Christian name. We kept all the names in the same formula, e.g. Rîmaru Ion, in quotations from official papers.

same bench as him.

Although we had been colleagues during the Lyceum, and we were colleagues again at university, Rîmaru tried to avoid me most of the time, especially when we were in a group with colleagues and women colleagues.

Sometimes when he needed money he came to me, calling for me from the hallway and asking for money, and, at the mutually agreed date, he would give them back to me."

(10th of June 1971, Militia file 751/B/1971, vol. 1)

Ioan Luca was another student who knew Rîmaru well, without getting close to him. He remarked on the fact that, even though they shared a room and went out together, Rîmaru always maintained his reserve. He mentioned also Rîmaru's reticence about women, a feature which became more and more pronounced.

Pitagora Constantinescu also shared a room with Rîmaru for about a fortnight in 1968.

"Rîmaru Ion had already repeated the year when he became part of the group I was in. I saw he was withdrawn and I put this attitude down to the fact that he had repeated the year. The professors asked us to get closer to him so that he would become more sociable. But, with all our efforts, we could not make him get together with us. He stayed like that, withdrawn, silent, and pessimistic.

Around the month of November, I went to sleep in that room, with him, Ciucă Constantin, and another colleague. I remember that he used to wake up in the night with such starts that he woke us up as well.

During the period of time I stayed in the room with him he was out many times. To be precise he went out around 11 pm, coming back in the morning around 4 am. Upon being asked where he was going, he gave evasive answers.

Normally he wouldn't return through the door. He knocked on the window, we would open and he would climb inside the sleeping chamber. We would get dressed and go to classes and he would either go to sleep or come to class later."

(29th of May 1971, Militia file 751/B/1971, vol. 1)

After Pitagora left the room, Ciucă told him that one night Rîmaru had become nervous about the noise coming from the next room, and begun to pace around. In the process he walked over a broken bottle which was lying on the floor, cutting his feet and legs, but without showing any sign of pain.

In another episode Rîmaru responded to the hazing of some colleagues who accused him of having syphilis by taking out a scalpel and cutting himself to show them that his blood was not syphilitic.

All of these accounts of Rîmaru's behaviour might have been the sort of stories which attach themselves to a character who was notably unpopular. On the other hand, the testimony of another couple, who knew him throughout his student career, was more targeted and illuminating, especially in regard to Rîmaru's attitude towards women.

Dan Dosinescu also came from Olt County. He was a year ahead of Rîmaru at the Institute, but he was happy, at first, to encounter another boy from the same region. They met casually on the campus, as students do, and became regular acquaintances.

> "In the beginning, Rîmaru was a communicative type, a good colleague, but I noticed along the way that he had started to become more withdrawn. We, his colleagues, put this attitude down to his failing to pass the year.
> Although I did not personally consider him a friend, I was surprised when he came to ask me, in the month of October 1970, to move into his room with him. I hesitated to reply. Furthermore, I asked my room mate – Cratov Vasile – to say that he did not agree to this. As far as I can remember, Rîmaru's room mate had agreed to this change because Rîmaru was treating him badly and he wanted to get rid of him."
> (2nd of June 1971, Militia file 751/B/1971, vol. 1)

Dan's evasiveness was based on something more than a casual distaste. By this time Rîmaru had alienated most of his colleagues, and Dan Dosinescu's girlfriend Doina Tămăşoiu is more explicit about her dislike and the reasons for it.

> "I became a year 1 student in 1967, Rîmaru Ion being in year 2. In 1968 the three of us became colleagues in year 2. During that time I did not have close relations with Rîmaru because I was in year 2 A, group 3206, and Rîmaru in year 2 B, group 3210. I can say I knew him only through Dosinescu Dan. In the years 1967

27

– 1969 Rîmaru was a quiet man, inclined to help out his colleagues with money. In the same time, he was not socially remarkable, I don't know if he had any friend or a relationship among the girls.

Starting from 1970 his attitude changed. I saw him with a preoccupied face, frowning, gazing downwards without looking at me, he didn't greet anyone and he had isolated himself completely. He was going around looking unkempt, had a tired look and was missing from classes, due to this fact he didn't pass the grade.

I want to note that during year 1 (1967) Rîmaru asked me about a colleague of mine, Rodica – now a year 4 student, whether she had any boyfriends. Because our relationship did not justify such a question, I gave him an evasive answer.

In 1968, around March, I was in the boys' hall of residence and Rîmaru came to me and asked, my boyfriend being also there, to go for a coffee with him. I did not like this thing at all, first of all because I was with Dan, secondly because of the manner in which he had approached me. I had never conversed with him, except on occasional meetings in the context of school. What struck me especially was his brusque attitude when Dan tried to explain to him that the normal conditions for this situation were non existent."

(1st of June 1971, Militia file 751/B/1971, vol. 1)

Another story which emerges from these early years, and, later on, was widely circulated, concerns the time when one of his neighbours in the student residence received a visit from a girlfriend. Rîmaru was thrown into a state of extreme tension and excitement by the event. He was unable to sleep and for the remainder of the night prowled around outside, 'like an animal', muttering to himself and staring fixedly at the window where he knew the girl to be staying.

None of this was lost on Rîmaru's teachers. The veterinary doctor Octavian Bica, workshop chief at the Faculty, took the opportunity to alert his parents.

"In the year 1971 the student Rîmaru Ion did not pass the grade and repeated year 3. I got to know him better on this occasion, noticing that he has an unsociable way of being and that his character is wanting, because he was coming to school messy, unwashed etc. On numerous occasions I told him to get a shave, but he invoked the fact that he'd had eczema on his face, saying that was the reason for not shaving.
With regard to his education, that area is also wanting. In the winter session he did not pass any of the three exams. In this situation I invited the student's parents over and discussed the inappropriate behaviour of their son with them. During these discussions Rîmaru Ion did not say a thing… I told him to start learning because otherwise he would be expelled. Personally, I have tried to make him be closer to me but he was impossible to understand. He used to lower his head, and stay silent. He led people to believe that he'd understood and then he did precisely what he wanted to."
(29th of May 1971, Militia file 751/B/1971, vol. 1)

Rîmaru had one obsession which escaped notice. The bus

and tram network in Bucharest was a perpetually moving river. Like the waters of the Danube, it carried a million strangers every day to destinations whose names were a half familiar poetry – Şoseaua Grozăveşti, Calea Dudeşti, Piaţa Dorobanţi, Piaţa Scânteii, Calea Victoriei, Gara de Nord.

On many of the nights when Rîmaru disappeared, and reappeared exhausted and fatigued, he was travelling, exploring the city from the solitary vantage point of a bus or a tram. This was how he came to know the city. Later on, it would be obvious that each of his crimes took place in the neighbourhood of a busy terminus, like Calea Dudeşti or the Gara de Nord, but for the moment his preoccupation with the transport system was a hobby, solitary and unremarked.

Chapter 2

It's the day of my mother
And all is full of bloom
I feel her presence here
As so many times before.

Gentle like a snowdrop
Her cheeks akin to tulips
Her scent is just like roses
This is how my mother is.

I love you, my dear mother
For everything you give me
I love you my dear mother
Just as you are.

I would like to give her a flower
That would resemble her
But no flower in this world
Is like my mother.

Mărțișor is the first day of March in Romania. By tradition it's also been a day devoted to women, who receive a gift of a double-threaded red and white string, together with a small trinket. This *mărțișor* is worn for the next week, on the lapel. In some parts of the country tradition dictates that the string would then be tied to a flowering tree, so as to bring good luck and a good crop. The colours, red and white, recall a time of pagan beliefs, red symbolising blood and death, and white purity and rebirth. Over the years, small charms and coins came to be attached to the string. Nowadays the charms take the form of flowers or animals, and can be made of a wide range of materials, from wood and plastic to silver, gold, and precious stones. As March approaches the *mărțișor* makers gather on the corners of the big public squares exhibiting their wares.

In a sense this is the tradition which reflects the ambiguous role of women in the society. On the one hand women were held up as heroines and role models. On the other hand women's bodies were seen as a commodity, but the narrative of women's dignity was pressed into service. International Women's Day on the 8th of March became the regime's flagship for women's issues, and its propinquity to the traditional celebrations meant that its official status could be underlined by the existing popular tradition. So the 8th of March became a day when women, especially mothers, could be lavished with small gifts.

This was an important strategy for the communist regime, because it offered them the opportunity to identify themselves with a popular symbolism, and to assume control of its direction and effect, which eventually climaxed in the role adopted by Elena Ceaușescu – Mother of the Nation. On the other hand, the symbolism wasn't simply an opportunity to hold special plenary meetings of the unions and the local communist organisations. There were other significant issues at stake.

To begin with, women had occupied a specific position

in a society where agriculture was based on small holdings. That was going to change substantially under the thrust of industrialisation and urbanisation. Women were about to play very different roles.

One issue, which was to have far reaching effects in this process, was the trend of population decline. After 1948 it was clear that all the populations in between Russia and Germany had declined dramatically. The same was true for those two giants, but in comparison they could, quite quickly, re-establish population numbers. On the other hand, all the countries in between their borders had suffered losses which it was tremendously difficult to make up.

In the sixties the Romanian government faced a declining population servicing an economy which depended on cheap labour and large internal markets. Women were the problem, that is, women who failed in their reproductive duty to the state. Women had a very clear role to play in the ideas fuelling the development of national communism, and Ceauşescu's anti-abortion legislation in 1966 forbade all forms of contraception. Women, therefore, were caught in between a modern post-industrial concept of femininity and the values of a peasant society.

Typically, several of the young women who were attacked and raped, were reluctant to declare the fact in their initial statements. Florica Marcu, for instance, only gave the final details of her horrific ordeal to the medical team who examined her later in the day.

"I have worked as a waitress at the student canteen since 1952. I know the majority of the students by sight, and too few of them by name. During the autumn of 1969 – I don't recall the day, I went to visit a friend of mine in Bucharest in order to watch the programme on the television. Around 9.30 pm I left my friend's place because I was feeling tired and I had to go to work the next day. While I was waiting for tram Nr 2 to arrive at Cişmigiu stop, I noticed I was being watched intensely by a young man. When I looked closer at him I realised he was one of the students who took his meals at my canteen, and later on I found out his name was Rîmaru Ion. When I looked at him he said *sărut mâna* (I kiss your hand) and I asked him if he was from the Veterinary School. At that moment he rushed at me and held me tightly by the right forearm. I freed my arm and didn't talk to him any longer. When tram Nr 2 arrived I climbed on board without noticing immediately that the young man had also boarded the tram. When I noticed it I asked him if he was going my way. He didn't answer but looked at me all the time.

When I got off the tram I noticed that the young man had also got off, starting to follow me. He was walking two steps behind me, without saying anything. During this time I tried to walk on other streets as well, around my home, because I was afraid that, if he saw where I lived, he would come the next day and break into the house. This chase continued until around 11 pm when I managed to hide in the middle of some cars which were parked, and I could see from there that the young man had lost my trail and was extremely desperate to find me. While he was following me I tried to tell him that I was living with my mother and that I was in no mood for what he wanted. But all this time he answered no word.

The young man was dressed in a suit of clothes of dark colour and had a ski-type coat on him, and had his hands in his pockets. The next day I told the other colleagues about what had happened, and my colleague Ciumenco Elena told me that the young man in question – after I showed him to her at the canteen – is a villain because she'd caught him on repeated occasions coming with fake meal tickets, and he swore at her once because she didn't give him his meal. I want to note that on the next day Rîmaru avoided me and didn't come to meet my eyes or to take his meal from my counter, as he did previously. After this incident, the same student, Rîmaru Ion, swore at the former administrator Dumitrescu because he didn't want to give him food without a meal ticket, saying that the administrator – meaning Dumitrescu – would die at his hands because he would not give up until he'd butchered him. After these threats they gave him his meal, but for around 30 minutes the student held his head in his hands without looking at the food and without eating, grinding his teeth, and afterwards he only ate very little."

(Ersebet Umbrich, student canteen waitress, born 1919. 1st of June 1971, Militia file 751/B/1971, vol. 1)

During 1969 Rîmaru's behaviour was becoming more and more strange and threatening, especially towards women, but he seems to have been able to maintain a regular routine. He went back to Corabia at weekends. During the holidays he worked on the docks, and, in his dealings with some men, he appeared to display a semblance of normality. This was the case with the surgeon and urologist Ion Prodan, who he met on the train to Corabia.

The surgeon lived in Corabia and was taking specialised classes at a hospital in Bucharest, between October 1969 and July 1970. He frequently travelled by train. Rîmaru approached him one day, at the Basarab station, and, claiming to recognise him, struck up a conversation. After this he encountered Rîmaru 3 or 4 times.

According to the doctor, the young man wasn't very communicative. The conversation would dry up, and he would sit reading the newspaper for the rest of the journey. On one of these occasions Prodan was shocked by Rîmaru's long hair and beard, and told him to shave and get a haircut, 'like normal people'.

This didn't discourage Rîmaru. Instead, he began to turn up, uninvited, at Prodan's hospital in Bucharest. On the first occasion he asked about a swelling on a joint of his hand. The second time he said that his penis was itching when he urinated. On both occasions the surgeon referred him to the student doctor. On another occasion they met in the street in Corabia. Rîmaru was on the way home from work, covered with dust and in a state of exhaustion. The doctor invited him home for a glass of *ţuică* and a meal. Seeing him devour the food the doctor realised how hungry he was. They met on one more occasion, when Rîmaru waited for him at the end of surgery and, again, showed him a scar on his hand, which the surgeon, once again, suggested taking to his doctor in Bucharest.

It seemed, from this acquaintance, that Rîmaru had a

need to confide in older authority figures. His attempts to receive treatment from Prodan appeared to be transparent bids for attention from the surgeon, which met with a blank wall. He now turned to confiding in his father. By this time, towards the end of October 1969, Florea was well established as a driver on the night bus through Floreasca. Rîmaru often visited him there, as well as turning up to travel across the city at night in his father's company. This was now his chance to unburden himself.

"In the past 2-3 years I discussed his relationships with women with my son, on several occasions, and he complained to me that he was not given any consideration by women, that he had no success with them. I gave him some advice."
(28th of May 1971, Militia file 751/B/1971, vol. 1)

Florea's advice seems to have taken the form of fixing his son up with various women. To his astonishment Rîmaru refused to meet any of them. In the first place Florea had proposed an arrangement with a girl, with whose mother he appeared to have come to an understanding. Ion would move in with the girl, with a view to getting married, and Florea would pay the expenses. Not surprisingly, Ion turned this down.

More worrying was the incident in Corabia when a friend of his young sister came to visit. Ion tried to get her alone in another room, but on each occasion the two younger siblings insisted on being present, frustrating his efforts to have sex with her. From that time Ion held a grudge against his brother and sister. When his sister visited him with a friend, he invited her in, but her friend had to wait outside, and, when the sister asked why, he replied, "What is the point of inviting her in?"

Florea tried to discuss all this with his son, but his investigations met with a blank wall.

> "In the discussions I had with my boy with regard to his relations with women, I recall he doesn't like to wait or to be postponed, but that he wished that, immediately after he met a woman, she would give in to him. I asked him why all this hurry and he said his blood was too hot, and that he felt this need."
> (28th of May 1971, Militia file 751/B/1971, vol. 1)

Florea persisted in proposing one woman after another, but for each one Ion found an excuse. When Florea suggested meeting a woman who worked as a cashier, he replied that she wouldn't look at him, because she had other men. In fact, Florea concluded, he had a bad opinion about women, who were 'generally perverse'. Florea was concerned enough to consult his son's attitude with Professor Cîmpeanu, his tutor at the university, and he received the advice which appeared to be the general solution to the problem. *Marry him off.* Ion's only response to his father's urgings to find a woman he could live with was to say –"What, do these women give in as fast as I want?"

In the end Florea was to discuss his son's behaviour with two doctors at the student clinic, but by then it was too late, and in any case their advice was something he'd heard before. *Marry him off.*

8/9 May 1970
Elena Oprea

It had been raining that night. It was now half past one in the morning. Elena Oprea had left the Pădurea Băneasa Restaurant where she worked and begun walking towards the Piaţa Sfântul Gheorghe. From the square she would usually take the night bus to the stop next to the Circul de Stat, and from there it was a short walk along the boulevard and into the cross street, Turnul Eifel, where she lived at Nr 40. She was known as Nutzi to her friends and family, and, on the morning of the 9th of May 1970, she was a week short of her 26th birthday.

It was a short journey, and in normal circumstances the square would have been crowded with traffic, but at this hour of the night there was hardly anyone to be seen. In any case, Elena was feeling uneasy. A week before this, she'd had a frightening experience. A young man had followed her, riding with her on the bus between the two stops. He had tried to talk to her, and then walked a short distance behind as she headed for her house. On that occasion she'd taken fright, hit the man with her handbag, and broken into a run. He'd disappeared, but the experience left her feeling threatened and vulnerable. Since then, her colleague Elena Ciobanu had taken her home by car. Tonight was the exception. She hadn't eaten at work, but she was carrying a white plastic bag with a freshly cooked steak, fries and some cheese. In her handbag she had her wages, because she'd been paid that day.

The houses in Turnul Eifel Street are large, two stories high, multi-occupied, with spacious yards, guarded by a high gate. Elena had reached Nr 40 at 2.20 am, and entered the courtyard, when she heard the footsteps behind her. In her agitated state she barely heard what the man said, but it was obvious that she was under threat. She screamed. At this moment, the assailant struck. Several heavy blows to the head with a metal rod. At the same time he stabbed her several times with a knife. Elena had no defence against this savage attack, but she screamed and screamed as she was bludgeoned to the ground.

At this point Elena's neighbours began waking up. Stoian Covatchev Ivanov heard a woman screaming and the dog barking in the courtyard. He imagined the dog had bit the woman, so he opened the door of the house and looked out to see what was happening. He saw 'some action' near the fence and concluded that 'the boys' – the tenants' children – were 'having some fun' with a woman. Covatchev stood there and watched, without making out much, for a couple of minutes. Then he heard the man in the yard throwing some objects on the pile of wood, then saw him dragging something big out the yard. At that point he heard the man say "are you dead?", before walking away. Covatchev went out into the yard cautiously, then approached the gate. The man was about 30 metres away, walking swiftly up the street towards the next junction at Ramuri Tei Street. Then he saw a woman on the pavement and realised it was his neighbour Elena.

He woke up the landlady Maria Santa. At this time Elena was still conscious, and she begged to be taken inside and put on the bed because she was dying. The neighbours dragged her into the house, and began cleaning the blood with water and vinegar. Another neighbour who had a telephone went to call the ambulance. This was at 3 am. The Militia arrived before the ambulance, which collected her at 3.30 am and got to the hospital 15 minutes later. Hours later Elena Oprea died.

Chapter 3

1/2 June 1970
Florica Marcu

During the beginning of June in Bucharest it was still raining unpredictably, and, although it was warmer, the strength of the wind made the streets inhospitable. The weather seemed worse in the north of the city, where Constantin David Tică Street is located, in a down at heel maze of little streets. This was a quarter which seemed to be left over from another version of the city, with giant housing blocks and the grime of an industrial complex towering to the north.

At half past one in the morning the streets were deserted. This wasn't an area which saw a great deal of traffic, in any case. The commercial lorries, which during the day criss-crossed the Calea Griviței, which was the main street leading to the factories, had thinned out to an occasional wagon, and the lamps along the smaller streets were dim and far apart so that the overall effect was murky and dark.

Florica Marcu was accustomed to the gloom, however. She was a waitress, 21 years old, separated from her husband and young child, and renting a room at a house in Constantin David Tică Street. She worked at night in the Mărășești Restaurant and this was the time she got home.

When she left the restaurant at around 1.30 am, she took

the night bus K to the Piața Sfântul Gheorghe to catch her next bus home. While waiting for the night bus U she met with an acquaintance who worked at the Cina Restaurant. The girl pointed out that there was a man staring at her, and, looking round, she saw that it was a man who had been following her on the other bus. She was alarmed, because the week before she had been followed by a young man on the night bus. He had stared at her persistently and then walked behind her, but she couldn't be sure it was the same man. In any case, when the bus U came and she got on, he seemed to have disappeared. Getting off on 1 May Boulevard, she noticed a militiaman doing his rounds, but she was in a hurry to get home, and she crossed the boulevard quickly. In Constantin David Tică Street she stayed on the lit side of the pavement. This was the right hand side. Her house, Nr 75, was on the left.

She was just opposite and about to cross the street, when she saw a man rushing towards her from the other side. It was the man from the bus K. Florica was now right opposite her house, in front of her neighbours at Nr 77. She screamed, before her attacker hit her a savage blow in the head with an iron bar. She collapsed and her assailant lifted her in his arms and carried her back along the road to the next cross street, Gheorghe Misail Street. Here he put her down under the cover of a parked lorry and, producing a knife, commanded her to take off her underwear. Dazed and confused she did what she was told. She noticed, however, that there was something odd about his face, and, after a moment, she realised that he was wearing a pullover, and he had stretched the collar to cover his mouth.

Ironically, there were several witnesses who heard a woman

screaming and dogs barking, and came out of their houses in time to see Florica, in the distance, being hit and dragged away from the scene. None of them called the Militia, or shouted, or did anything else to scare the attacker.

Viorica Bazavan, living at Nr 77, was up with a sick child, preparing tea. Her husband, Nicolae, tried to go out but she stopped him, and went out herself, together with her mother Eufrosina. At the gate, they saw a man hitting the woman, in the distance. Then they met with Cezar Ionescu, an 18 year old Lyceum student who lived at Nr 84. Maria Gelea at Nr 82 came out on her porch to enquire, then went back to bed with her husband who she couldn't wake up. Florica's landlord, Traian Piso, heard the commotion but was frightened to go out because he was an old man.

Between them, all that these witnesses managed to do was collect Florica's belongings, which were lying scattered on the street, and check her ID. After this they spent about 15 – 20 minutes in the street talking, and, since no one had come out of Nr 75, they threw her things into the courtyard. Then they went back to bed, or continued watching the street through their windows.

In the meantime, the attacker had picked Florica up again and was carrying her, this time to the Sfânta Vineri[5], a cemetery which stood at the centre of the maze of streets. At this point he put her down and, gesturing with the knife, urged her to climb over the fence. She tried, but in her battered state she could hardly do more than paw at the

5 In Romanian mythology, Sfânta Vineri appears as an old woman endowed with supernatural powers. It is believed the origins of this myth lie in the cult of the Roman goddess Venera. However, in the Romanian Christian Orthodox tradition, Sfânta Vineri refers to Saint Paraschiva, whose name (Paraskevi) means Friday in Greek.

wall. Seeing this, he half pushed, half lifted her over the fence, shoving her so vigorously that she fell a little distance away on the other side, landing headfirst on a tombstone, where she lay semi-conscious.

Her assailant leapt over the fence and, picking her up, led her to a freshly dug grave, decorated with a large cross. He forced her to kneel and then, standing behind her, made her swear that she would take him as a husband, that she would tell no one about the events of that night, and that she would meet him again. She agreed, mumbling the words quickly. Then he made her take the rest of clothes off. Now, completely naked, she lay on the tombstone while he had sex with her. He took his time, running his hands all over her body, and finally biting her on the buttocks and the left thigh, before he was satisfied.

Eventually, it came to an end. Florica had now recovered her senses, and, desperate not to anger her attacker, she meekly climbed the cemetery fence when ordered. They walked back towards Constantin David Tică Street, but when they got to the junction, the man stopped her. He compelled her to stretch out her arm, which he stabbed three times, after which he sucked the blood. While doing this he made her promise to come to a meeting next day, at 2 o'clock, outside a well known clothing store in the centre of the city. By this time Florica would have agreed to anything, and she did so, without thinking about the strangeness of the request. After this, the man appeared to be walking her home, and bleeding and half naked she walked in a daze along her street towards her house. Suddenly, a vehicle appeared, heading down the road towards them.

It was a Carpați lorry delivering newspapers, but Florica

didn't have the time to notice this. Without thinking, she dashed into the middle of the road, waving. The driver, Ioan Vladu, pulled up in time, astonished by the appearance of a bloody, half naked scarecrow of a woman, almost under his wheels. "Help me. Help me" was all she could say at that moment, and she tried, frantically, to point to her rapist. But, by this time, the man had started running, and in the time that the truck driver could look around he had vanished round the corner, like a shadow in the night.

In the early hours of the morning, right after the attack, Florica was taken to the Militia station where she received "medical attention". Then she went with the militiamen to show them where and how she was attacked. In the cemetery she recovered her wedding ring from near the tomb where she was raped. Then they took her to the hospital. She only declared that she was raped when she encountered the medical team who examined her, and later she said it again in the statement she made the following year.

19/20 July 1970
Theft at Calea Rahovei

Ion Rîmaru's university year ended at the beginning of the summer in 1970. He had failed the year and been told that he would have to repeat it. He was in despair, but for some reason he didn't go to Corabia immediately. Instead, he stayed in Bucharest, at student accommodation on Mărăşti Boulevard, near the Arcul de Triumf, in the north west of the city. On the night of the 19th of July 1970, he walked through the city, going from the Arc to the Calea Rahovei, in the south west, the further end of the city. No doubt he was looking for women to approach, but, if so, he didn't find any. At 2.30 am he found himself outside of the clothing store OCL Confecția.

Calea Rahovei is the main thoroughfare leading into the city from the South. During the day it is crowded with commuter and commercial traffic, but at that time of night it was deserted. There was no one to see. Picking up a stone Rîmaru smashed the display window, climbed in and took a striped suit, two jackets, one in a navy blue fabric, the other in brown and yellow checks, and a pair of beige coloured trousers. Then he travelled back to Mărăști Boulevard, carrying his loot.

A couple of days later he packed the suit and one of the jackets, and went to see his father at his workplace in Floreasca. He said that he'd bought the clothes from someone, but Florea, who, after all, was partly supporting him, was sceptical. Eventually Ion admitted that he'd stolen the clothes, and Florea agreed to keep them. A couple of months later Florea returned the package.

This became a pattern. In the months to come Florea was to be more and more involved in laundering the proceeds of his son's crimes, and in advising him about what to do with them.

It was a difficult time for Ion. Later on, talking about this period, he describes how his

> "state of despair had reached a maximum because of the exams, because of my pecuniary situation, and because of the environment I was living in at the university, where everybody held me in contempt,

including the professors and colleagues."
(Rîmaru's appeal, 13th of September 1971, File Nr
3900/1971 of the Tribunal of the Municipality of
Bucharest)

A few days after the theft of clothes in Calea Rahovei, and
before he left to work in Corabia, he tried another robbery.

24 July 1970
Margareta Hanganu

Margareta Hanganu (age 19) worked at the shoe factory
Flacăra Roşie (the Red Flame) in Bela Breiner Street. On the
24th of July she was working the 2 pm to 11 pm shift. She
left the factory at 11 pm together with 46 year old colleague
Ileana Cioric and they walked towards Foişor Street. On the
way Ileana Cioric jumped on bus Nr 35 leaving Margareta
to enter Foişor Street alone. In any case, several workmates
from the shift were walking behind or in front of her. Foişor
Street is a little street in the centre of the city. In 1970 it was
a busy quarter dotted with restaurants. Margareta Hanganu
walked along, clutching a bag which contained a pair of
shoes and a small sum of money. The street was dark, and
she was unaware that there was someone hidden behind a
parked lorry. When she walked past the vehicle, however, he
emerged, and came up behind her. It only took a few steps,
because she looked around in a fright, before the assailant
struck her on the head with a metal bar, pushed her, grabbed
the bag out of her hand and ran away. She ran after him,
intent of recovering her stolen bag, but, as she ran, two
colleagues, Vasile Iordan and his wife, came up behind her

on a motorcycle with a sidecar. Seeing the blood on her face and clothes, they stopped and took her to the nearby Caritas Hospital.

One year later, Margareta Hanganu identified Rîmaru as her attacker from his photograph, before picking him out from a Militia lineup.

A few days later Ion left for Corabia. He would spend most of the summer working, but once he was back in Bucharest something had changed, and the crimes he was now to commit in a period of seven months were more horrible and more frightening than anything he had so far attempted.

Part 2

Chapter 4

Bucharest in the Seventies

At the beginning of the 1970s, the locals of Bucharest had been thinking of themselves as prisoners in their own city. The most critical period had been in the 1950s, when the simple fact of being dressed elegantly, or daring to wear a hat were sufficient reasons to be arrested and disappeared. Even women were not allowed to wear hats, only batik headscarves. Men had sold their suits in the markets a long time ago. They did not need them anyway. The fashion was for overalls and Stalinist sandals.

Things were timidly changing in 1970. The Red Army had left Romania, and even Soviet advisors were retired at the beginning of the 1960s. The greater part of the political prisoners had been freed, and they were returning home, many of them marked by years of torture. The restraints were no longer visible because the enemies of the people had been eliminated.

The old and charming part of the city persisted in existing. The historical area had not disappeared, and it was still alive. The narrow streets, paved with cube shaped stones, with tram lines running them, cut across the city. Lipscani, Covaci or Smârdan, the same streets which pre-dated communism, continued to represent the commercial hotspot. Calea Rahovei and other middle class neighbourhoods, ordered and civilised, still had the same character. The houses had shops on the ground floor, and on the top floor were the rooms of the owners, typical of the small entrepreneur at the start of the 20th century, who aspired to the middle classes. The traffic from the city had started to get busy, but the locals still liked to walk in a city which was familiar.

The Skoda Karosa buses, called Skoda Cazan (Skoda Cauldron), with undulating sheet iron and leather seats, were painted in a joyful colour combination, red and white or yellow on top, but they seldom reached their stops and gave the commuters headaches. In the normal way of things, the young, the old, women, children, all clung to the doors because they had no more room inside. Public transport worked day and night, and the tickets were cheap.

At the beginning of the 1970s, before the regime's cultural revolution, the young were looking for good times. The children of the nomenclature could be seen alongside foreigners in hotels, discothèques and night bars. Middle class youngsters contented themselves with student clubs or cultural centres. The options were limited, and freedom of movement reduced and controlled. The good side was the fact that young people felt relatively secure on the streets. Criminality and lawbreaking had decreased significantly, and the stories about ferocious criminals of the past had disappeared from the collective memory of the locals.

Balaurul (The Dragon) and his rival, Sandu Moise, nicknamed Hitler after his moustache, the leaders of rival gangs in Bucharest, were now forgotten. Armed with Soviet-made automatic weapons, they had started a bloody war between their groups in 1945, because Hitler had stolen Balaur's girlfriend. Now, at the beginning of the 1970s, the complicated war years, which had revealed the capital's shadowy underworld, were a distant memory. Barely remembered also was Petre Silberschmied, aka Argintaru (Silversmith), another famous bandit who had left behind him scores of dead policemen. He used to rob banks and stores and took a special pleasure in waging war on the authorities. He was arrested after he sacrificed his entire gang during one attack, and he died in 1945 trying to "escape" from police custody.

Such gangsters had been eliminated by the incorruptible commissioner Eugen Alimănescu and his brigade of 22 young policemen, which he had called Fulger (The Lightning). Alimănescu was nicknamed the Iron Commissioner, and was assassinated by the Russians after he discovered a ring of jewel thieves run by Soviet officers.

But these days when gangsters controlled the city's neighbourhoods were gone. Now, the terror came from the authorities themselves and no one dared to be complacent in the adventurous and opulent life of a criminal. From time to time, rumours about a ferocious murder appeared in Bucharest which, in the relatively safe climate, would become well known among the city's inhabitants. Such subjects were, however, ignored by the press because they were on the list of those forbidden by the censorship.

22/23 November 1971
Olga Bărăitaru

Olga Bărăitaru was manager of the Uranus buffet. This was in Uranus Street at the centre of the urban quarter which would later be demolished to make room for the House of the People in the dictator's policy of urban systemisation. As a result it was a popular and thriving venue. On the night of the 22nd of November it was hosting a christening party. The weather was bad. There had been showers all day and by the time the party ended it was raining buckets.

At 2 o'clock in the morning, 47 year old Olga Bărăitaru was on her way home in a car driven by Gheorghe Gheorghe, husband of one of the employees, Ana Gheorghe. They dropped her, as usual, in the Păcii Boulevard, right in front of the block of flats where she lived on the seventh floor. Clutching her leather overcoat around her, she ran into the building. The lift was out of order and she resigned herself to climbing the stairs.

She got no further than the second floor. A man was hiding on the landing and, as she came past, he leapt out and began hitting her on the head with an iron bar. Later on, Mrs Olguța, as the neighbours called her, couldn't remember what happened, and it was clear that she was too dazed to defend herself, or to do more than scream.

The attacker dragged her back down the stairs and out to the front of the building. By this time a number of her fellow tenants, the nearest being Eugenia and Mihai Redai, had heard the screams, but the noise stopped as abruptly as it had begun, when the assailant started hitting her again.

He then dragged her round behind the block of flats, to the stairs leading down to the basement and bracing her half conscious body against the basement door, began ripping off her tights and underwear. Then he raped her, while all the time she moaned loudly. It was these moans which probably saved her life.

The apartments in that wing of the building extended

from front to back, so that one of the families, the Redais, who had been awoken by the screams, continued to hear a woman moaning in the rear of their flat. Their bathroom window actually overlooked the basement stairs, so the wife switched on the light and peered out to see what was happening.

The rapist saw the light come on and ran away, taking with him Mrs Olguța's bag, which contained a small sum of money and a pair of spectacles. She lay where he left her, in a pool of mud and water, until 7.22 am, when, after a complex series of negotiations with the Militia, she was taken to the Dr Gheorghe Marinescu Hospital in an ambulance.

Some months later Ana Gheorghe saw Rîmaru's photograph in the newspaper and made a statement to the effect that he was a regular at the restaurant – a familiar face.

Later on the case of Olga Bărăitaru posed certain puzzling questions. Rîmaru confessed to the crime, but, rather than hiding on the landing, he claimed to have attacked her in front of the building. In the bag he claimed to have found 2,000 Lei instead of the 500 Lei the victim claimed to have lost. He claimed also to have followed her before the attack when she ran away and jumped onto a tram.

It is possible that he was confusing various different incidents and locations, which might mean that he was responsible during this period for several more attacks, which were not reported or identified by the investigating team. His own account is typically baffling, and led the investigators to conclude that he was deliberately confusing events in order to construct a defence based on the idea that he was the victim of his own urges.

"Following the exams period at the end of 1970, and after I had a meal at a restaurant near the Veterinary School, I followed home one of the waitresses. She was living in a block of flats on a big boulevard with buses and trams. Some days later I happened to be in that area in order to meet a girl – to be more precise, I was actually looking for a girl that I had met previously. It was late at night. I didn't find that girl I was looking for. It was raining and all of a sudden I saw in front of me that woman from the restaurant. I tried to speak to her but because she started to scream I hit her with the metal rod with grooves – presented here in the court. I hit her several times but didn't think she could die as a consequence. I hit her in the head. After that I took the victim in my arms and went to a place not far from her block, near a house, and raped her. I took her bag in which I found 2,000 Lei. When I approached this victim initially, a couple of days earlier, after I had followed her, I asked her to come with me but she ran away and jumped into a tram."

(1st September 1971. File Nr 3900/1971 of the Tribunal of the Municipality of Bucharest)

One of the most worrying aspects of the case, however, was what it revealed about the citizens' view of the authorities and its effect on their relationship with each other and with the state. A reconstruction of the witness statements tells the whole story. Mrs Olguţa was attacked around 2 o'clock in the morning. Like many of the other victims, her ordeal was happening within earshot of several occupants of the building. Afterwards she lay there, moaning, for something like five hours before anyone came to her assistance, and then it took the Militia nearly an hour to react. At the same time it is also obvious that, after the event, everyone felt a sense of shame, and they were eager to excuse their lack of response by blaming their desire to be on time for work, or a Party meeting, or their household duties.

Witness statements taken on the 2nd of July 1971
(Olga Bărăitaru case)

Mihai Redai
"I live in 166 Păcii Boulevard, at the ground floor of block 36. During the night of 22/23 November 1970, after we went to bed, we heard two screams of a woman. Lifting my head off the pillow I saw that the head of a person was passing under the window. I couldn't tell if it was a man or a woman because I was just waking up. I woke up and looked through the window but couldn't see anything. Looking at the clock I noticed it was 2 am. Because our daughter was pregnant my wife went to check on her. She was sleeping so my wife went to the bathroom and turned the light on. Returning to bed she said 'who knows what drunkard passed by the window', after which we went back to sleep.

Around 4.30 am, when I woke up to prepare for work, I entered the bathroom where I heard a prolonged moan. I washed up and dressed. I didn't go to check who was moaning out there, although I could hear it right at the back of my apartment. I can't explain why I didn't go.

My daughter, Stoica Florentina, also woke up and I told her about the moans I had heard at 2 am and at 4.30 am and she then said that she was afraid to go out of the block. At 5 am I went out of the apartment together with my daughter. There was no light in the lobby or on the inside staircase, but I could see on the entrance steps – near the door – a pool of blood. I avoided the pool of blood together with my daughter and walked her to the tram stop. When I returned I saw on the alley, at about 5 metres from the entrance of the block, a woman's shoe, and near the steps there was another shoe – a woman's shoe as well. I entered my apartment and told my wife, Redai Eugenia – that I saw a pool of blood in front of the block and two woman's shoes, also telling her that we should alert the Militia and the *Salvare* (ambulance).

My wife told me to go to the office and take care of my business, and she would wake up my son in law Stoica Alexandru. I left for the office at 5.30 am. I don't know what happened afterwards. I also want to point out that, when my wife told me to go to work, she also said that she would wake up my son in law in order for him to wake up another neighbour as well, named Vasilescu, to go and check who's there and alert the Militia. I mention that I didn't go to check on who was there in the back of the block, near the flat where I live, because I was in a hurry to go to work."
(2nd of July 1971, Militia file 751/B/1971, vol. 4)

Alexandru Stoica
"I live in 166 Păcii Boulevard, block 38, on the ground

floor, apt. 44, together with my parents in law Redai Mihai and Redai Eugenia. My wife, Stoica Florentina, and I sleep in the room on the corner of the block.

On the night of 22/23 November 1970 I heard no noises and no screams. Around 5 in the morning my father in law Redai Mihai came into my room and told me that when he went into the bathroom to wash, around 4.30 am, he heard somebody moaning behind the block, on the stairs to the basement that corresponds directly to the bathroom window.

I went there and looked down the bathroom window but because it was dark outside I saw nothing. The bathroom window is very small. Then I went back to sleep.

I mention that when I looked down the bathroom window I heard somebody down there, near the wall, moaning several times, and I went back in and continued sleeping. I didn't go out because I had no reason to.

After my father in law Redai Mihai left for work with my wife Stoica Florentina, my mother in law Redai Eugenia came into my room around 5.45 am and told me to get dressed and take another neighbour called Vasilescu so we can see who is outside and call the Militia.

I got dressed and called at Vasilescu Aurel's door, he got dressed as well and we went together up to the first floor, to the Pătrașcu family who have a telephone. The husband, meaning Pătrașcu Dumitru, opened the door. Vasilescu Aurel told him that there was somebody moaning behind the block and asked him to call the Militia. Pătraşcu Dumitru answered that he didn't know the number for the Militia and he closed the door.

We came down from the Pătraşcu family and went behind the block, to the place where the moans were heard. We did not go down that stairway to the basement, which is a little sloping, but stayed on the pavement, and looked from there and saw somebody who was moaning continuously. It was at a distance of some 5 metres from us. We didn't go to see who it was. We went to the public phone at entrance Nr 1, and at about 6.05 or 6.10 am we called the Militia.

A platoon leader (*plutonier major*) from the Militia came immediately and he went in to see who it was. He told us it was a woman who had been hit on the head. The platoon leader went back to the Militia Station Nr 16 and came with a Militia captain who stayed there, and the platoon leader left in the Militia car, with the woman being left where she was.

In the end I went to the place where the woman was, with the captain, I kept a lantern in my hand, and the Militia captain went to the woman who was lying there, asked her who she was, how did she end up down there, and the woman could not talk, she was bloodied all over the head and the body. I went out with the Militia captain from the basement stairway and, around 7 am he made a phone call to the ambulance, which came at 7.22 am.

The ambulance came, the woman was taken away from there and put inside the ambulance, but she had not been identified, I didn't know who she was."

(2nd of July 1971, Militia file 751/B/1971, vol. 4)

Cornelie-Marie Pătrașcu
"On the morning of the 23rd of November 1970, at
5.30 am, two neighbours called at the door of the flat
where I live, Vasilescu Aurel and Stoica Alexandru.
My husband Pătrașcu Dumitru opened the door. The
two asked my husband to allow them to make a phone
call to the Militia, because there was a dead woman
behind the block, in the rubbish area.
My husband said he didn't know the number for
the Militia and the two left. I was annoyed that
my husband was not very amicable, to the extent of
allowing the men to make their phone call. Around
6.15 am I heard the door bell again. I went to the door
myself and I saw it was the rubbish man, I don't know
his name, who asked me to go to the 5th floor and put
back the covers from the light bulbs there, which were
taken out and laid on the flower pots. He came to me
because he knew I was the person responsible with
managing the block, but I didn't go because there was
no hurry to put the covers back at that time.
At 7 o'clock, after my husband left for work and
the boy for his school, I went out to see what had
happened. I went behind the block and I found, on
the stairway leading to the basement, Vasilescu Aurel,
Stoica Alexandru and somebody from the Militia,
who had a lantern.
I didn't go down the stairs, which are sloping, but I
stayed on the pavement. I could hear moans and I
asked whether they had called the ambulance. They

told me they did. I went back to the apartment and I also called the ambulance myself, at 7.05 am. At 7.20 am the ambulance came and transported that woman to the hospital. I did not recognise her, she was very bloodied and disfigured. I know that it had rained during that night. Around 8 o'clock I found out that the victim was Bărăitaru Olga, occupant of the block in which I also live myself."
(2nd of July 1971, Militia file 751/B/1971, vol. 4)

Elena Grecu
"I live on the ground floor of block 38, right at the entrance on the left hand side. The Redai family lives on the left. On the night of 22/23 November, I don't know what time it was, I was woken up by a scream, saying "aaargh". I also heard somebody banging on the door of the lift. I cannot say if it was before or after the screaming that I heard the banging on the lift.
I did not attach any importance to this, believing it was the neighbours from upstairs, as for the lift people bang on the door almost daily. We went back to bed and fell asleep again, until the morning I did not know what had happened. Around 7.20 am I heard people talking in front of the block and then I looked in and asked what had happened. A neighbour, namely Stoica Alexandru, told me that a woman or a girl was behind the block at the rubbish area, beaten up."
(2nd of July 1971, Militia file 751/B/1971, vol. 4)

Eugenia Redai
"I live in 166 Păcii Boulevard, on the ground floor of

block 38. On the night of 22/23 November 1970, after we went to sleep, I heard around 2 o'clock somebody passing by the window to the back of the block, and they screamed 3 or 4 times.

I would like to note the screams were quite loud and sounded terrified. Because my daughter was pregnant and was going to give birth, I woke up and looked inside her room, but they were sleeping. Then I went and turned the lights in the bathroom, which corresponds with the window of the stairway that leads to the block's basement, stairway which is sloping. I heard no other noises then, and together with my husband we went back to sleep.

Around 4.30 am, my husband woke up so he could get ready to go to work. He went in the bathroom to wash himself and when he came back he told me that again he heard those screams or moans, imagining it might be a mute woman, and thought we should call the ambulance. I told him to go to work, and that I would wake up my son in law Stoica Alexandru. I woke up my son in law and he went and woke up another neighbour, Vasilescu Aurel.

Both of them went up on the first floor to make a call from the Pătrașcu family's phone. He didn't allow them to make a call, but I don't know why. Then they went to the public phone where they called the Militia, which came immediately. I didn't go out to see what had happened, except when the ambulance came. On the morning of the 23rd of November 1970 I also saw a pool of blood on the entrance stairs to the block, in the direction of my apartment."

(2nd of July 1971, Militia file 751/B/1971, vol. 4)

Dumitru Pătrașcu

"I work at the TB dispensary of sector 6, as a medical statistician. On the morning of the 23rd of November 1970, around 5.30 am, two inhabitants of the ground floor, whose names I don't know, called at my door. I opened it, they told me they had found a dead woman behind the block, at the rubbish area and asked me to make a phone call to the Militia Station Nr 16. I told them I did not know the number for the Militia and that I didn't have the necessary time to call them, reminding the two that there was a public phone at entrance Nr 1. The two left.

During the night I heard no noises and no screams. Around 6.30 am I left for my work. I mention that it was dark in the hallway and on the stairway. In the hallway there was a militiaman with a lantern, and on the entrance stairs to the block, on the last step, I saw a big bloodstain. I did not go to see what was behind the block, as I was risking being late for work."

(2nd of July 1971, Militia file 751/B/1971, vol. 4)

For whom the bell tolls...

There is a question which emerges from all this. How can a number of women be attacked within earshot of several witnesses, without any more than cursory interventions? Studying the files at this distance, it is clear, in hindsight, that several of the assaults could have been stopped several times by even a tentative approach.

The answer lies in the Romanian reluctance to get involved in things that do not concern them directly, especially if they have an unpleasant or disturbing aura about them. The reluctance is even greater when those matters might lead to further involvement with the authorities. In any case the first port of call would be the Militia.

In 1970 militiamen were ubiquitous, but distrust in their services was equally ubiquitous, and they were generally greeted with fear or suspicion. There were a multitude of jokes illustrating popular attitudes towards them. For instance – why do you always see three militiamen together? Answer – one can read, one can write and the third has to keep an eye on those two dangerous intellectuals. Or, a helicopter crashed in a cemetery. The Militia came to the incident and opened an investigation: they discovered 800 victims!

Such attitudes were based on the history of the force's organisation. The communist regime abolished the Police in 1949 and replaced them with a General Directorate of Militia. In addition to fighting crime, the new force was responsible for common law offenses and the control of road traffic, tasks which involved the surveillance of the population. The Militia granted internal visas with the aim of following and controlling the way in which the population moved. It also assisted the Securitate in dealing with the deportation and repression of the remaining anticommunist partisan groups. In the 1950s, no Romanian could move from one locality to another without the permission of the Militia. Travel abroad was strictly forbidden, without the backing of the Securitate and the Party, so the Militia was also responsible for preparing lists of suspect individuals.

All this meant that the traditional apolitical and experienced policeman became an object of suspicion, and the forces began to be purged. Former policemen were jailed in the Făgăraş penitentiary, 'the policemen's prison', together with former soldiers and employees of the secret services.

The new militiamen were vetted for their loyalty to the regime, with Party workers and people from a proletarian background being prioritized. In the popular narratives of books and cinema the former police forces were presented as corrupt and criminal. In comparison, the militiaman was seen as intelligent and able, fair without abandoning the guidance of the Party, and the terror of criminals everywhere.

Romanians knew that there was an enormous gap between this image and the truth. By 1970, patterns of recruitment and training were changing, but the 20 year history of the force had left an indelible imprint.

In a society in which the forces of law and order were an instrument of oppression for a long time, the level of trust people have in them is very low. These were times when a black car could stop in front of any building, a few men could call in unannounced and go away dragging someone with them. In the circumstances, people felt that the less contact you had with the authorities, the better.

There are also circumstances to do with the details of life in a state with restricted amenities. In a typical housing block there might be only one or two families with a phone. To have someone knocking on your door at five in the morning for permission to use it would have been a distinct annoyance.

Finally, having a dead person near the house immediately

made one a witness for the state, meaning you had to deal with the Militia and other officials, with all the risks that involved.

In the Olga Bărăitaru case we see people going to work, knowing something horrible has happened, but motivating their refusal to deal with the problem by saying that they risked being late, or that they had a Party meeting to attend.

Good Samaritan attitudes were few and far between. If you heard someone moaning it might have been a drunk, and who cares about a beaten up drunk. He probably deserved it.

A good boy...

Although it appears that Rîmaru was driven and confused, he was, nevertheless, assembling the tools and cultivating the methods which facilitated the rampage that was coming. From the previous year, Florea, his father, had been living for some time with Filareta Călin, and Ion's first visit to their home was on the 25th of December 1970, Christmas Day. She and Ion didn't hit it off. Filareta was an assertive 44 year old, and it was clear to her that Ion was not interested in having a relationship with her. He came twice a week for a meal, between 10.30 pm and 12.30 am, he never addressed her willingly, and, whenever she was present, turned his back on her.

On top of all this he frequently asked his father for spending money in addition to the money he already received for his accommodation and meals. Given Florea made no contribution to the household expenses, it was not a happy situation. When Florea brought his son's laundry home, Filareta told him point blank that she had no intention of "washing the clothes of the son."

Worse was to come. One day Florea came home with a hatchet wrapped in newspaper in his briefcase, which he said belonged to Ion. Towards the end of February 1971, Ion came to the house when Florea was at work, and asked for the hatchet, saying that he was leaving for Corabia and wanted to take it home. When Florea came home Filareta asked him whether Ion had visited him at work. The answer was no. Then she told him about Ion coming for the hatchet. Florea's response was to put his face in hands and say, "what is this all about taking it to Corabia? I told him to leave it alone."

In fact it was clear that by this time Florea and Ecaterina had serious concerns about Ion's behaviour. Round about this time he told his father that he had an "unfortunate fate" and that he had "no place on earth", but he didn't say why.

He had shared a room with Constantin Ciobanu until November 1970. Then he had lived with Ionel Matei until January 1971, and finally he shared with Constantin Năcuță, who, after one month, refused to stay, blaming the fact that Rîmaru was a somnambulist. After this Rîmaru lived alone, and although he asked his fellow student Dan Dosinescu to share with him, Dosinescu refused. From that time on the only persons with access to his room were his parents.

When Ion came back from Corabia after the summer, Florea noticed that he was carrying a knife with a horn handle, in a leather holster. He said that he had bought it from a sailor. Florea forbade him from wearing the knife, but, during the month of February, when he visited Ion's room, he found the knife hidden among other things on a locker. It seems that he found the hatchet at the same time and questioned his son about why he needed the weapons, to which Ion replied that he needed them to defend himself.

According to Maria Murăruş, the administrator at the Nicolae Bălcescu Institute, Rîmaru was a "closed in character", who was isolated from the other students. From the month of February when he was left by himself in the room, he placed a padlock on the entrance door and the cleaning was done by janitor Luiza Bucur only in his presence, because he refused to give her a key. Maria did notice one change. Rîmaru was now better dressed.

On holiday in Corabia in the February of that year his sister noticed a new isolation about her brother. "He talked little, did not salute the neighbours, went out of the house very little, and his gaze was much changed. My grandmother asked him what was the matter with him and advised him to go see a doctor, but he replied there was nothing wrong with him."

Florea told Ecaterina about the discovery of the knife and the hatchet and said he would confiscate them from Ion. He also said that Ion wandered all over the city at night, "like a vagabond", and at this point he wondered whether Ion had committed some crime, because of the rumours around the town about several murders. Ecaterina discussed this with her son. When she asked why he walked around at night, he replied that he was going to a girl's place. Unconvinced, Ecaterina persisted, but Ion refused to say anything further, apart from declaring that he had been cursed not to have a place among people. Then she asked him the crucial question. Was he the perpetrator of the murders that people were talking about? His expression changed, and he told her not to look at him, because he was not a good boy any more.

Chapter 5

Rumours in the night

In the Romania of that period, 1970, the entire press, central as well as local, were characterised by two methods of selecting what could be printed: censorship and propaganda. All the classic means of media information, newspapers, publishing houses, television and radio, were completely controlled and permanently under surveillance.

The role of censorship was to eliminate from society all the information that did not fit in the patterns dictated by communist ideology. On the other side of the coin, propaganda filled the void left by censorship with information which had the semblance, but only the semblance, of truth. The communist regime, therefore, maintained itself in power by the use of both censorship and propaganda. Yet the system, as vast as it was – having behind it numerous institutions and thousands of party activists that constituted this filter – convinced no one. Romanians knew about the existence of censorship, even if the government denied its existence, and, as for propaganda, it was the source of much Romanian humour, with every official claim being recycled as a joke.

The goal was to re-educate the population, and to focus attention on the basic tenets of communist ideology. This task was the responsibility of the General Directorate of

Press and Printed Materials (*Direcția Generală a Presei și Tipăriturilor*), assisted by various sections of the party for Propaganda and Agitation, or by the Press sections. These functioned both centrally, in Bucharest, and locally, within all the party organisations in the country. This monopoly of information meant that it was a simple matter to filter public messages and transmit only those that were agreeable to the regime.

At the same time, propaganda had to fulfil another task: building the cult of Nicolae Ceaușescu and his wife, Elena, as well as constantly feeding it with new elements.

The press was forced constantly to broadcast texts written by propagandists, about the dictators' glorious past, about their courageous fight with the inequalities of the previous regime, about their remarkable activities in the present. All this was invented, however, and no one believed it.

It was not permissible to publish criticisms of the regime, which was considered irreproachable or, at the least, on the road to perfection. If there was something to criticise, it could only be published with the approval of the party leaders, most of the time with the approval of the Ceaușescu family. The system, however, was never criticised. It was people who were criticised, those people that the party was preparing to punish.

In these circumstances the circulation of newspapers went down. The government's response was to oblige people to subscribe. Romanian Television, the only TV station, which appeared in 1959, had ended by broadcasting 15 to 30 hours per week, most of it dedicated to political propaganda. The few entertainment shows broadcast on Saturdays and Sundays were awaited impatiently and viewed with pleasure.

The only successful newspapers were the sports journals, but the propaganda chiefs immediately noticed their importance, so that *Sportul* (The Sport), the best selling sports paper, was under threat unless its first 3 or 4 pages were filled with articles about the Ceaușescu family, and about the sporting credentials of the communist party.

Obviously, the censorship did not encourage articles about criminals and law breaking. It was considered that in socialist society there were no crimes and no criminals, or at least such events did not happen often, and were not done by the working people, or by the studious youth. Instead, crimes were committed by a few unbalanced elements who did not understand the principles of communism.

When, after long periods of time, such misdeeds occurred and the censors allowed publication of the news in the press, the report took the form of a sort of moral: there is still among us, comrades, a lawbreaker, a criminal, a wrongdoer, but now he pays for his deed!

Films or plays broadcast on television told almost the same story, under a different guise. A young man comes out of the prison after serving his punishment, usually a theft or a thoughtless murder, and tries to reconstruct his life by finding a place of work and establishing a family. Society and the Party were disposed to offer this man a second chance, to re-educate him and transform him into a new man.

Scânteia (The Spark) was the official newspaper of the Central Committee of the Romanian Communist Party, and it was the first daily to publish the most important news. *Scânteia* also offered the official journalistic point of view on any event on which press analysis was allowed. Other newspapers followed the lead. *Scânteia*, in other words, was the spearhead of the propaganda effort.

The newspaper offered political information and articles about Ceaușescu, written in wooden language, and alienating the reader. Readers were, however, attracted to the second page of the newspaper which had a dedicated section called *Faptul divers* (Diverse facts). The section occupied only the top corner on the left of the page and contained, as a rule, four or five very short articles of crime reports, fires, and investigations into the state enterprises which were the followups to anonymous letters – in short, what we call investigative journalism. On the other hand, the series of crimes associated with Rîmaru were ignored by the journalists of *Scânteia*, including those who assembled *Faptul divers*.

Another widely read newspaper was *Informația Bucureștiului* (The Information of Bucharest). This was the official voice of the Municipal Party Committee and of the Bucharest Popular Council. Unlike *Scânteia* or the other central newspapers, *Informația Bucureștiului* had a relatively heterogeneous air, lots of politics, but also articles about entertainment in the capital. But during the years 1970-1971, the period when Rîmaru was active, *Informația Bucureștiului* did not publish one item of news on his crimes.

The situation didn't change even when the Militia realised the murders seemed to have an identical modus operandi and concluded that the killings were committed by the same author. The view of the investigators that they were on the track of a serial killer took shape after the murder in the night of 8/9 April 1971, which took place in Vulturi Street.

In the days following, when the authorities should have told the locals to take precautions, the press, including

Scânteia and *Informația Bucureștilor*, was full of news about the 24th congress of the Communist Party of the Soviet Union in Moscow. Ceaușescu was leading the delegation, and the newspapers were inundated with official photos of the delegates.

In any case, a serial killer and a sadistic rapist without scruple could only exist in the depraved Western societies, not in communist Romania, not in Bucharest. Nevertheless, the locals were more and more concerned. They had found out, by word of mouth, that a murderer was killing and raping women, while the Militia and the Securitate seemed helpless.

Paradoxically, although censorship did not allow the publishing of information about Rîmaru's murders, about the places in Bucharest where victims had been found, or about the ferocity and cannibalism of the murderer, the news was circulating fast. Rumours went around and alarmed the city. In the conversations taking place between locals, there was almost always somebody who had a connection with the story itself. This made him or her extremely credible as a source, more credible than any article that might have appeared in *Scânteia*, because the last victim was either a work colleague of a friend of my mother, or the murderer was seen in the night by the neighbours of a friend of mine…

The authorities could not stop the spreading of the rumours, and, in a way, they did not want to. The Militia felt the need to communicate with the public in order to mobilise it, but in this goal it realised that the press would be unhelpful, to say the least. As a result it decided to transmit the information to the public directly, through the militiamen who were sent to walk the streets and to gather data on the ground.

Chapter 6

15/16 February 1971
Gheorghița Sfetcu

People, he's killing me…

Gheorghița Sfetcu was 19 years old, and she worked as an assistant waitress at the Odobești Restaurant in Calea Moșilor, a major thoroughfare in the centre of Bucharest, not far from the central University Square. On the 16th of February 1971, she left the restaurant at 2 o'clock in the morning, and walked across the Piața Sfântul Gheorghe to catch the bus which travels all the way along Șoseaua Giurgiului, one of the major gateways to the south of the city. In terms of Bucharest travel, it's a long way, and it takes about half an hour to get to the Piața Progresul (rebuilt since that time), which was her next stop.

From here on, she walked through the side streets. At half past two in the morning it was cold and damp. When she reached the intersection of Farului Street with Torței Street – where she lived – she saw a man standing with his back to the street sign. As she approached him, he covered his face with his hand and took a step towards her. Paralysed with fear she had the presence of mind to scream, "people, he's killing me". At this point the man jumped on her and hit her several blows on the head with an iron bar.

The screams woke Ilie Marin who lived in the front of the building facing the spot. He got up and turned the light on. This was enough to alarm her assailant. He stopped hitting his victim, and ran, taking her handbag which contained a small sum of money.

She came to her senses, lying in a pool of blood, on the pavement. She struggled to her feet, picked up her shopping bag and gloves and, in a state of confusion went towards her home. All the while Ilie Marin watched her go, staggering and unbalanced, but he had no idea what happened, and he went back to bed. When Gheorghița got home, she told her husband, Constantin, that she had been hit by a citizen on the corner. Then she lapsed into a coma.

Constantin alerted the Militia, who went to the junction of Farului and Torței streets, where they found several traces of blood, a rubber heel broken off the victim's boots, and several small coins.

In the meantime, Gheorghița Sfetcu, in a grave condition, was transported by ambulance to the Dr Gheorghe Marinescu Hospital where she underwent emergency treatment.

16/17 February 1971
Elisabeta Florea

On the 17th of February 1971, it rained, and it was still raining heavily at 4 o'clock in the morning. Elisabeta Florea, an 18 year old assistant waitress, was on her way home after work at the Vulcan Restaurant, near the Gara de Nord station. She was single, beautiful, and she lived on Banul Antonache Street with her sister Floarea, a worker in a cotton factory.

She had left work together with two male colleagues and they travelled by night bus to Piața Sfântul Gheorghe. They parted there and Elisabeta took bus B towards the Floreasca area. She noticed a young man get on the bus at the second stop, at the same time as two transport workers. The young man didn't buy a ticket. Instead, he showed a bus pass, with a picture, to the *taxatoare* lady sitting at the back of the bus. He remained standing in the back, while Elisabeta was in the front of the bus, sitting behind the driver. She got off at the Piața Dorobanți and walked for 200 metres towards her house.

She was moving as quickly as she could go, head down and hunched over against the torrential rain. She was halfway along Ștefan Negulescu Street when the young man who had been on the bus appeared behind her, grabbed her by the coat and spun her around. He shouted at her, "*Stai să-mi bat joc de tine, ori te tai*" (Stay put so I can have my way with you or I'll cut you). Once he was facing her, the man gripped her by the lapels of her overcoat with his right hand, and with the other hand drew a knife. Elisabeta screamed for help, but at the same moment she was slammed against the gate of the nearest house, Nr 29, and stabbed 14 times in the head, the hand and the right leg. He stopped only when the occupant of Nr 29, Nicolae Popescu, who had been awoken by the screams, threw up his window and shouted "*Ce faci mă, o omori?*"(what are you doing, *mă*[6], are you killing her). Immediately, the man gave up his attack and fled the scene.

Left to herself, Elisabeta took refuge in the Popescus' courtyard. There was a bench at the back of the yard and

6 Informal mode of address, with the version *măi*.

she sat on it, trying to recover her strength. No one came to help her, until a police car appeared, followed by the ambulance. Popescu only came out of the house when the Militia arrived.

In the meantime, Elisabeta's older sister, Floarea Florea, was waiting for her at home, only a few streets away. She wasn't worried because she imagined in the appalling weather Elisabeta might have remained to sleep over at some acquaintance's house.

As a consequence of the trauma she suffered, Elisabeta was committed to the Emergency Hospital, requiring 7 days hospitalisation plus another 10 days to recover from the loss of blood. She had been saved by Nicolae Popescu's intervention, and by the thick clothing she was wearing, which partly protected her from the blows of the knife. After the attack, she gave up her job at the Vulcan Restaurant and retired to her village in Argeş County.

Later in the morning (7.55 am) Ion Rîmaru went to the emergency room of the Plastic Surgery Hospital for treatment to cuts on his little finger and ring finger. During the next few months he asked a number of people, fellow students, the surgeon he met on the train, and his parents to help him look after the wound, and ended by committing himself to hospital a couple of months later.

4/5 March 1971
Fănica Ilie

Fănica Ilie worked at the Vulcan Restaurant. She was 31 years old, married, with a 4 year old daughter, Mariana. On the 5th of March she left the restaurant in the early hours of the morning, and set out for Scărlătescu Street, which was only a short distance away off the Banul Manta Boulevard.

There was still snow lying thick on the side streets, but that was not the only reason for Fănica's unease. Since the attack on her workmate Elisabeta Florea the restaurant had been buzzing with rumour and speculation. She, herself, some weeks previously, had been followed and accosted by a young man, so she waited for another waitress who was going the same way and they only parted when she was a short walk from home; but she was hurrying as she left the relatively well lit boulevard and turned off into her road.

Scărlătescu Street, in those days, was lined by two storey houses, set back from the street, and mostly separated by a narrow courtyard, guarded by a gate. The assailant was waiting, concealed behind the gate of Nr 46, an old house with an upper floor and an attic.

As Fănica approached, he struck her a heavy blow on the head with a metal rod, and she fell to the ground. He dragged her unconscious body inside the courtyard of the building going right to the back of the block. Then he placed her face up and started to undress her violently, slashing and ripping at her clothing.

He pulled open her outer clothing, her overcoat, her pullover and her blouse to give him access to the lower part of her body. He slashed her skirt, ripped her suspender belt, lifted her camisole up above her nipples, raised her brassiere above the breasts, and ripped the rest of her underwear, tossing them beside the body. Then he raped her unconscious body. This was the first opportunity in which the killer could indulge himself with the unconscious and passive body of one of his victims, and he took full advantage. He bit her on the breasts and on the thighs, tearing off chunks of flesh, leaving traces of semen and marks of his teeth. Before he left, he took her wristwatch, and her bag.

In the morning of the 5th of March 1971, when the occupants of Nr 46 came out to shovel the snow, they discovered the body of Fănica Ilie, half naked and mutilated, as the killer had left her. The Militia were called, and they turned up with a police dog, named Beri, who failed to locate any sign of the murderer.

The murder of Fănica Ilie, however, was a turning point in the response of the Militia. They had no way of making a firm connection between the various crimes being committed, but they now set to work to find the perpetrator using the only solid evidence they had - blood and the marks of the killer's teeth.

The Militia developed a working hypothesis about the perpetrator of the crime. They were dealing with a) a thief who was also a rapist, b) a violent psychopath, armed with weapons, or c) a repeat rapist, mentally ill, a sexual pervert. Accordingly, the Militia ended by interviewing more than 300 mentally ill people. After the next murder, when they decided they were dealing with a serial killer, they re-interviewed a number of people including the ex-boyfriend of Florica Marcu, who she initially accused before withdrawing her statement.

For the moment, the Militia had no idea about how to go about catching the killer, a fact which contributed to the hysteria of the exercise mounted during the month of April – Operation Vulturul.

In the meantime, Rîmaru was now almost completely cut off from contact with the people around him. Around

March or April, Florea went to pay for his food and lodgings and met with the administrator who told him that his "son was mad, that he cut himself with a knife, that he had no friends or woman friends, and that it would be good to *marry him off.*"

When Florea heard this he confronted Ion (again). Ion said that he had cut himself on a window. Florea swore at him and accused him of lying, because the woman janitor and another colleague had seen him and told the administrator that he'd cut himself with a knife. Ion denied it again. Then Florea examined the hand closely and saw that the little finger had seemed to be healing. Looking closer he saw signs of cuts in the palm. The upshot was that Ion said he intended to commit himself to hospital for an operation to heal the stiffness of the little finger on the right hand.

Part 3

Chapter 7

8/9 April 1971
Gheorghiţa Popa

Gheorghiţa Popa worked as a waitress and cloakroom attendant in the Prietenia Restaurant in 11 Iunie Street. She was 35 years old, dyed her hair blonde, and everyone called her Geta. She was divorced from her first husband Gheorghe Wolff, and married to Constantin Popa, but they didn't live together. Instead she lived at 55 Vulturi Street with her friend Pia. Gheorghiţa's 9 year old daughter also lived there. She'd had a history of abortions and gynaecological problems, and she had recently split up with her boyfriend, Paul Bădeaţă, a projectionist at Cinema Central, who happened to be working on the evening she was attacked.

It was about 2 o'clock in the morning of the 9th of April. Geta had been at work on her feet for 8 hours, and she had just passed the junction of Traian Street into Vulturi Street. As she went past Nr 40, Rîmaru attacked, showering her with blows from a hatchet and a knife to the head and the upper body, wounding her 48 times. Then he dragged her into the courtyard of Nr 40. Her shoes came off, and he threw them away somewhere. He also took the wristwatch she was wearing, which he kept until the moment of his arrest. In the courtyard, he positioned her near a tree, ripping and slashing the underwear, tights, shirt, blouse and brassiere. Then he raped her, while she lay dying. It is not clear at what point she actually died, but in the process he bit her on the breasts, and kissed her on the vagina, which he also bit, leaving a piece of flesh in his mouth.

In a later confession Rîmaru says that he walked around the streets looking for women. At a certain point, he met a girl on a street, and upon telling her what was it he wanted, she laughed and went inside a building. A short while after this he met Geta. He asked her to go and sleep with him, but he was refused, pushed and hit. When she tried to run, he hit her on the head several times, with the hatchet-pick, and she fell in the middle of the road. He continued to stab her with the knife all over her body, striking her wherever he could, because he was incensed by her rejection, and in order to revenge himself on women because they made fun of him. After he was finished, he left, and entering another courtyard he washed his hands and clothing. Afterwards he fled the scene by taking a *getax*[7] to the vicinity of the hall of residence, where he wiped the blood off his clothes.

Operation Vulturul

In April 1971 the authorities began to study, in comparison with the cases of Elisabeta Florea and Gheorghiţa Popa, all the unsolved cases of murder or attempted murder on record. In the light of this survey the investigating team concluded that the cases of Elena Oprea and Olga Bărăitaru had the same perpetrator, and the Militia began to work on the basis of the theory that Oprea, Marcu, Bărăitaru, Florea and Popa were all attacked by the same man.

---

7 Bucharest taxi.

The new hypothesis immediately generated a number of new suspects, including boyfriends and acquaintances of the victims. In particular, Florica Marcu fingered a former lover and he remained a suspect until after Rîmaru's arrest, when she admitted to having made a mistake.

The authorities also decided on a new strategy, entitled Operation Vulturul after the street where Popa had been attacked. Vulturul meant 'eagle', and the exercise implied a massive increase in surveillance. Six thousand men from various law-enforcement agencies patrolled the streets of Bucharest each night, as well as 100 cars and 40 motorcycles. Medical personnel, night bus and tram operators, hotel and bar employees were all mobilised, in a state of high alert.

To complicate matters, the Militia had to work with the Securitate. The operatives of the General Direction of the People's Security (*Direcția Generală a Securității Poporului*), protected the state against foreign intrigue. The Securitate suffered from the same problems of recruitment and training as the Militia, but while the Militia inspired suspicion and contempt, the Securitate inspired fear. If the Militia arrested you there was a chance that you'd be released quickly. With the Securitate there was no such prospect. So it was unlikely that Operation Vulturul would engage the participation of the public. The upshot, however, was to create an atmosphere of nervous anxiety and fear, which did little or nothing to catch the killer. In the end, over two and half thousand arrests were made, and over eight thousand individuals were stopped and had their IDs checked, but Rîmaru managed to attack several more women, and commit another murder, before he was trapped by a piece of traditional police work.

From the 12th to the 26th of April, Rîmaru committed

himself to the Plastic Surgery Hospital for an operation. The damage to his fingers, sustained during the attack on Elisabeta Florea in February, had been treated on the morning of the 18th of February, but the wounds had re-opened during the attack on Gheorghiţa Popa in April. Operation Vulturul was supposed to gather all the information about the persons who presented themselves at surgeries and hospitals with wounds caused by cutting or piercing. For some reason, no one reported Rîmaru, even though he returned for a check-up and treatment on the 29th of April, the 3rd and the 5th of May.

This is more surprising because Rîmaru attracted a lot of attention. Nicolae Virgil Onaca, the surgeon who operated on him in April, testified that -

> "...during hospitalisation, as well as after it, in ambulatory treatment in the emergency room of the hospital, the collaboration with patient Rîmaru was very difficult, if not impossible, because, contrary to medical indications, the patient was removing the wound dressing and sutures himself, and did not respect any medical instructions given to him. It has to be mentioned that, during all the time I've known him, the patient Rîmaru was unkempt, unwashed, unshaven. In my discussions with him I noticed things that I remarked upon in the presence of the other patients, namely that Rîmaru was violent and irascible."
>
> (5th of July 1971, Militia file 751/B/1971, vol. 4)

Domnica Bejenaru, a nurse in the unit, also testified to

Rîmaru's peculiarity.

"He made the impression of a strange man. He was very agitated, was waking up at night all the time, saying he could not sleep, and sitting on a gurney on the hallway, smoking. I asked him a few times if I could be of any help and give him a sedative, but he refused saying they didn't do him good. Of all the medical personnel he only allowed me to administer two injections with penicillin. He was quiet, did not talk to anybody on the ward. He had a way of being rough with the medical personnel, recalcitrant. I saw him once eating a piece of salami which he did not cut as it would have been normal, but was biting off the whole piece. Once, I needed a knife and a patient from the ward addressed me loudly and said the student had one. Rîmaru, without me asking for anything, took a very sharp knife from a bag and gave it to me. I even made a joke at the time, saying that a man could shave with that knife."
(3rd of July 1971, Militia file 751/B/1971, vol. 4)

Although it was clear that Rîmaru wouldn't or couldn't modify his behaviour, he had the presence of mind to get his parents to destroy the evidence connecting him to the attacks.

"After a while, looking for him at the university and not finding him there I imagined he committed himself to the former Emergency Hospital on Architect Mincu Street. I went to the hospital around the dates of the 15th or the 16th of April 1971, around 10-11 am, I talked to him and he asked me to go to the residence and pick up some things and wash them at home. I went and I picked up from his room a white lab coat, 2 shirts (one grey, the other light blue), a pair of Chinese long johns, the striped pyjamas in grey and blue, a navy coloured ski fabric coat, and a trench coat in dark beige, and a men's suit in terylene colour green. I mention that my son asked that the suit of clothes and trench coat I should take to clean at *Nufărul*, and the rest of the things I should wash at my place.

When I picked them up I saw that there were a number of bloodstains on the Chinese long johns, the right leg as I remember. Also, on the trench coat – beige – there were several stains of oil, whitewash, paint and bloodstains. I noticed the bloodstains on the right hand side of the trench coat, at the front. The trench coat was soiled with blood, as far as I could ascertain, on the front as well as on the lining. The suit was also soiled, as not to be wearable, but I did not notice bloodstains. Also, I did not notice bloodstains on the two shirts that I picked up from the room where my son lived. The navy blue coat in ski fabric, which I picked up from my son's place, was dirty, very dirty, impossible to wear, but I did not notice bloodstains on it. I want to mention that I picked up all these things from the locker in the room where my son lived, with the exception of the navy blue coat in ski fabric and beige trench coat, which were hanging on the coat rack in the room. The other objects had been placed in disorder in the lower part of the wardrobe I mentioned. The clothing items I enumerated above were dirty, leaving the impression he had rolled on the ground dressed in them.

I picked up these items on the date of the 15th of April, as far as I remember, and I remember because it was on the same day, before going home, that I left the suit of clothes for the purpose of cleaning to a *Nufărul* unit near the ITB Floreasca Garage. The other items of clothing I took to my house in Bucharest, and I asked my mistress, Călin Filareta, to wash them, but she refused, affirming that she "does not wash the dirty stuff of the son".

When I left on my leave that I spent in Corabia, I took with me these items in order to wash them in the family, together with my dirty items, and I told my wife as well as my mother in law to wash them. I don't know which one of them washed them out. It is certain that, upon my return to Bucharest, I brought back all the things mentioned above, clean. I want to note that I did not bring back the flannelled long johns considering they were no longer necessary because it was warm.

After my return from the provinces, the next day, meaning the 22nd of April, I went to the hospital where my son was committed, and took foodstuffs to him from the countryside. On this occasion, I asked the boy why the clothing was so dirty, and he said he rolled around with a woman who angered him because she refused to give in. Upon being asked about the bloodstains on the items of clothing, he replied that he had cut himself with the knife "because he felt like it, having too much blood". I insisted with this question but he gave the same reply – that was what he felt like, to cut himself, and he showed me marks of cutting, both at the left leg in the lower part and at the right leg in the lower part. I recall 3-5 cuts on the right leg and a single one on the left leg.

At the end of the month of April or beginning of the month of May, I don't remember exactly, I took both the suit of clothes from *Nufărul* and the other items of clothing that had been washed in Corabia to the hall of residence where my son was accommodated. I want to mention that during the course of the month of February or March, current year, on the occasion of a visit I made to my son's room, in his presence, I noticed a cut from a hatchet, or to be more precise the mark of a hatchet on the table that was in his room. I got upset and I asked what that was about, and he answered he got angry and had hit the table with the hatchet. I asked him where did he have a hatchet from, and he said that he had found the fire-fighter type hatchet, but he did not say where he found it."
(28th of May 1971, Militia file 751/B/1971, vol. 1)

In hindsight Florea seems to be trying to distance himself, in his statement, from his son, but his tone is consistent, and supported by his wife and his mistress. In her own statement Filareta Călin reports that Florea told her that Ion went so far as to cut his penis in order to reach orgasm. Referring to his visit to the hospital, she reports Florea saying that, when he reproached Ion about committing himself for the operation and abandoning his studies, the boy replied "to leave him alone, and if he doesn't like it, he can disown him."

This was in April, and events were due to accelerate relentlessly, and, although he didn't know it, Rîmaru only had a few short weeks of freedom left.

Chapter 8

1/2 May 1971
Stana Sărăcin

Stana Sărăcin was a tram driver at the ITB Depot Bucureștii Noi. She finished work at 12.45 am and left the Depot Bucureștii Noi with the night bus to Piața Chibrit from where she made her way on foot along the 1 May Boulevard.

When she reached Nr 339, a thin young man about 22 years of age, with an elongated face, wearing side burns, appeared in front her, and asked what the time was. Stana looked at her watch and saw that it was 12.55 am, but the young man, without saying a word, reached out and gripped her crotch. She slapped him in the face, and he looked around, and then hit her a heavy blow with his fist. Dazed, she fell over on the grass sidewalk, and started to cry out for help. The attacker leaned over her, but just then a voice was heard from a balcony shouting "what do you want with that woman, *mă*". On hearing this, the young man got up immediately and ran away through the side streets behind the block.

The person who shouted from the balcony was witness Paul Misai, who confirmed that, on hearing a woman's screams, he looked down in the street and, at the corner of his block, in the intersection with Cașin Street, he saw a woman fallen on the grass walk and, near her, a young man, who ran away the moment he shouted at him.

Stana Sărăcin subsequently made a complaint at the Militia Station Nr 17. When Rîmaru was first questioned, he described the attack, without mentioning Paul Misai's intervention, claiming that she started screaming when he made his proposition, after which he hit her on the head with an iron bar and then left. His account was linked, however, to Stana's complaint, but she couldn't pick him out definitively in the ID parade, and Rîmaru subsequently denied that he was the perpetrator. There was no doubt however about his next victim, and it was this next attack which yielded up the vital clue which was to prove his downfall.

4/5 May 1971
Mihaela Ursu

Mihaela Ecaterina Ursu, also known as Pusi, was 39 years old, and an assistant in the Optics Department of the Faculty of Physics in the University of Bucharest, working for a PhD. She lived in a university apartment on the third floor of 4 Rotundă Street. She had been married at 35 to Alexandru Ursu, nicknamed Dudu, who was studying in the evening at the Faculty of Constructions, and worked in a factory.

She was an animal lover who kept 7 cats, which she boarded out nearby in the Calea Moșilor; and there were another 3 cats and 3 dogs who lived at another address. The couple's mother in law lived with them, and complained that she was dirty, didn't wear a bra, didn't contribute to their expenses, and slept at odd hours. Her husband proposed a separation, but she promised that she would return to normal life after she finished her doctorate. In the meantime she couldn't work at home because of the mother in law, so she stayed late at the university, studying. In fact it was pure bad luck that Mihaela found herself where she was at that time of night. She had spoken to an old family friend, Elena Mureşanu earlier on in the evening about 11.30 pm, and then called again at ten past midnight. Elena asked where she was calling from, and she said that she was still at the university, but she was going to visit the cats on the way home. Elena looked at her watch and warned her about going out on the street at that late hour when it was raining and with so many killings going on. Mihaela said that she was very angry because the people where she was keeping the dogs wanted to rip her off, because they wanted more money. She asked Elena for advice and promised to visit in a couple of days. Elena advised her to go home.

By this time, Operation Vulturul had ensured that everyone knew about the serial killer, and the only women on the streets at this time were women whose occupations forced them to travel home late at night – waitresses and transport workers. Mihaela was an exception. She was an independently minded academic, who, according to Elena, had only two passions – physics and animals.

It was raining heavily. Sometime after 1 am Mihaela was walking along Stupinei Street, dressed in an overcoat and with an open umbrella. A man approached her and she tried to evade him by turning into the courtyard of Nr 24A, at which point he struck her several blows over the head with an iron bar. They struggled, she screamed, and he cut her throat with his knife. He then lifted her up in his arms and took her to the back of the courtyard. She was wearing a chemise, a shirt, a skirt and an overcoat. He cut them open, and ripped her underwear off, tossing one of her stockings aside. Mihaela was now dead. He positioned her face down, her lower torso raised by a pile of bricks. Then he raped her dead body.

While he was occupied in this way, he heard someone entering the courtyard, so he jumped the fence and ran away. In fact, it was Vasilica Neagu, a bus conductor, who was coming home from work at around 2 o'clock, and, ironically, she entered the house without noticing anything unusual. The next day, traces of blood were found on the stairs of her house, and it was established that the shoes she was wearing that night had bloody soles, explained by the fact that, when she entered the courtyard, she stepped in the blood.

Paraschiva Dumitru and Aurelia Maghiar who lived in the same apartment confirmed the times, stating that, before Vasilica Neagu arrived, they had heard several moans but they did not realise where they were coming from. It wasn't until forty minutes past five in the morning that Paraschiva Dumitru opened the kitchen window, and saw the body behind the block. On her finger was a wedding ring, inscribed 'Dudu'.

Operation Vulturul had created a new urgency. The Militia logged the call at 6.20 am. By 7 am the investigation had begun. In attendance were Prosecutor Vasile Comşa from the Prosecutor's Office of Bucharest Municipality, Lt. Col. Ioan R Constantin from the Criminology Institute, Lt. Col. Corneliu Serboteiu from the Criminology Service, Mjr. N Ghircoiaş from the Judiciary Service, Mjr. Stan Moroianu from sector 3

101

Militia, and Dr George Rafa, medical-legal expert.

Their memorandum goes into fearsome detail about the circumstances of the killing. They found a trail of blood leading to the body. They found a pair of abandoned shoes, and a handbag with blood and hair sticking to the bottom. In the bag were personal items, including rent receipts and ID cards. There was also a postcard from Dusseldorf. In the plastic bag she was carrying were –

> "three candles of artisan type, red, blue and white; three plastic bags with alimentary leftovers; a yellow coloured plastic flagon, empty; a red coloured plastic flagon, empty; a small statuette in rubber representing a dwarf; a grey umbrella holder, alimentary leftovers in a preserve tin, and a knife for opening preserve tins."
> (Memorandum, 5th of May 1971, File 751/B/1971, Prosecutor's Office, Bucharest Municipality)

They found, also, a bite mark on her neck, and a strand of her assailant's hair entwined in her fingers. Finally they found a "ticket", soaked in blood and unreadable, except for the heading.

Later on Rîmaru, in his confession, said that he was carrying a kitchen knife and the iron bar. He reached the Traian neighbourhood, and tried to accost an unidentified woman who laughed at him when he asked her for sex, and entered a courtyard. Immediately after this he spotted Mihaela.

Chapter 9

4/5 May 1971
Maria Iordache

"The undersigned is Iordache Maria, daughter of Ion and Florica, born on the 3rd of January 1929 in Bucharest, divorced of Cristescu Alexandru, a mechanic at Electrical Works Grozăvești. I have 7 children, 4 of whom are minors, all under my maintenance. By profession I am a tram driver at Giulești Depot, non-committed politically[8], living in 31 Bălăcescu Radu Street, sector 7.

I declare the following:

On the morning of the 5th of May 1971, around 4 am, I left my domicile going to work. From Bălăcescu Radu Street, I went out on Sidefului Street, then on to Teslui Street and I went on Basarabescu Street circa 50 metres after which I veered to the left on to Mehadiei Street. I walked on the pavement on the side of the ICEM factory, which is on the pavement on the left, up to Alboteanu Street, when I was hit on the head to the right side, and then I started to run and to scream, during which time I received more blows.

I ran for some 30 metres when I heard an iron falling

---

8 Not a member of the Communist Party.

on the pavement. At that time, out of instinct, I turned my head and saw a citizen dressed in overalls and worn overall trousers who leaned forward to pick the iron up. I crossed Mehadiei Street, and ran on Nucșoara Street, and entered a courtyard about one house on the right. During all this time I screamed for help. When I reached the bottom of the courtyard, and I saw he wasn't coming after me any longer, I looked in the street but I did not see that citizen anymore."

Maria subsequently went to the nearest Militia station and came back with Major Marin Pană, who retraced Maria's steps with her, followed by platoon leader Ion Bour and the dog Torel, but the rain had washed away all traces, and there were no witnesses. She was transported to the Dr Gheorghe Marinescu Hospital where she was treated and released.

Rîmaru also confessed to this assault, saying that, on a rainy night in May, he left the hall of residence carrying the iron bar. He went first on Șoseaua Giulești to an uncle of his, but finding the gate locked he went away, and subsequently saw a woman who he asked to go with him. She screamed and he hit her on the head with the iron rod. She ran away and screamed, but he continued to hit her and she managed to escape only due to the fact that he dropped the iron and she entered a courtyard. Unlike Maria's description, he was dressed in a navy blue ski coat, and not overalls.

On the 5th of May, following what had now become his usual pattern, Rîmaru went looking for medical attention. Sofia Badea, who worked as a nurse in the Trauma and Plastic Surgery Hospital, remembered the occasion.

"On the 5th of May 1971 he presented himself with a very dirty wound dressing and, when I took the bandage off, I saw that the operated wounds were forced, better said stretched, which made me signal to Dr Onaca that the patient did not respect the restrictions imposed.

Rîmaru Ion presented himself in a very sloppy condition, full of mud on his clothes, and you had the impression he was a drunk who, while under the influence of alcohol, rolled around in mud. Dr Onaca drew his attention to the unkempt attire and also to the fact that he did not respect the indications given after surgery. On that occasion I found out that the young man was a student of veterinary medicine. In order to justify his unkempt attire, Rîmaru said he had performed surgery on a horse."

(3rd of July 1971, Militia file 751/B/1971, vol. 4)

Later on, Maria was responsible for one of the stranger aspects of Rîmaru's trial. In September, she was still suffering the after effects of the attack. "I am in a very bad state, I shake and I cry and all the body feels faint and I forget things easily as, for example, if I set to do something one day, the next day I forget what I was supposed to do."

By then, the investigators had charged Rîmaru with all the crimes which bore significant similarities to the more notable cases. On the other hand, she had been unable to pick out Rîmaru from photographs or from the ID lineup. Studying the newspaper reports of the trial, however, she identified Florea Rîmaru as her assailant. The authorities couldn't substantiate the claim, but it was partly responsible for Florea's subsequent arrest, and for the cloud of suspicion which surrounded him until his death.

The Militia were now following various lines of enquiry. One was the bite marks left on the victims. Professor Petre Firu at the Institute of Criminology examined the traces of bites in the cases of Fănica Ilie and Olga Bărăitaru, and concluded that they were made by the same man. He outlined the assailant's anthropological type and his typical physical characteristics. The anthropologist Dr Cantemir Rișcuția, based on these descriptions, constructed a drawing of the criminal, with a high level of resemblance noted after Rîmaru's arrest. So, early in May, there was a probable portrait of the offender.

Second was the high probability that the killer's clothes had been stained with blood. An exhaustive list of cleaners was questioned without success. Unknown to the Militia they were on the right path. Florea had attended a meeting of the Militia with the staff at his garage, and he must have had a sound suspicion about Ion's activities. The result was that officers only discovered after the arrest that when Florea had Ion's clothes cleaned at *Nufărul* he now used the pseudonym of Florea Vrănescu.

Third was the likelihood that the killer had injured himself and would seek treatment, which he actually did. Unfortunately, no one reported this.

The note that had been left under Mihaela's body seemed like a dead-end. Examined under a sodium lamp at the Students Hospital it revealed only some numbers and an unreadable text. For the moment, therefore, it remained in a drawer, unread.

6/7 May 1971
Margareta Enache

On the night of 6/7 May 1971, around 2.30 am, the Militia received a telephone call from Ioan Vinersar, watchman at the Tailoring Cooperative *Muncă și Artă* (Work and Art). A woman had been attacked by an unknown person in Porțile de Fier Street, in front of building Nr 39.

On the scene, the militiamen found the victim in the tailoring workshop of 74 Porțile de Fier Street, where she had been taken by Ioan Vinersar for first aid. She was in a coma, identified from the documents she had on her person as Margareta Enache, waitress at the Select Restaurant, living in Bucharest, 48 Porțile de Fier Street, sector 2.

Immediately after this, the victim was transported to the Emergency Hospital I.C. Frimu, after which she was sent to the Institute of Stomatology where she also received specialised assistance, then was committed to Dr Gheorghe Marinescu Hospital, with the diagnosis of "cranio-cerebral and facial trauma with wounds to the face and tongue, dental fractures, left temporal and occipital wound with caved fracture and cerebral hernia".

According to the watchman Ioan Vinersar, during the night, around 1.15 am, he saw a thin brown haired young man passing several times in front of the tailoring workshop, and, after a short time, a young woman he knew by sight passed by as well. In about one minute he heard a scream.

When he went out in the street, he saw the young woman fallen in front of Nr 39, and near her was the person described above, holding an object in his hand. At the sound of the watchman's whistle, this person threw the object he held in his hand in the courtyard of the building and ran away.

When the ground was searched, the objects thrown in the courtyard of the building Nr 39 turned out to be the victim's umbrella and bag. No other clues were found due to the fact that it rained heavily during the entire night of 6/7 May 1971, flooding the street.

About 60 days later, the victim Margareta Enache had recovered enough to be interviewed. She picked out number 1 and 12, pictures of Rîmaru, from a set of 17 photographs. This was the person, she said, who she had seen in the garden of the Select Restaurant where she worked, a little while before the attack.

The hatchet he used was found on his person at his arrest, together with the knife that caused the wounds to the victim's mouth. In his confession he claimed that he did not have sexual intercourse with the victim, because a citizen, the watchman Ioan Vinersar, had appeared.

6/7 May 1971
Elena Buluci

A couple of hours after the attack on Margareta Enache on the 7th of May 1971, Elena Buluci was on her way to work in a restaurant in the Gara de Nord station from her home in 17 Amiciţiei Street. She was carrying an umbrella, a handbag, and a plastic bag with her work clothes and other things in it. She got off at the Carpaţi stop in Calea Griviţei around 3.45 am. A thin young man, wearing a moustache and dressed in a beige trench coat and a grey hat, also got off. It was raining heavily and she went into the entrance hall of the flats next to the station, to shelter from the downpour. The young man also came with her. In a short time she saw a tram coming, which she rushed to get on, but it stopped only briefly and she didn't catch it. The young man followed her, standing only a few feet away and staring at her insistently. She looked up and down the road to see if there was another bus coming but there was nothing. After a while, she realised that the next bus was late, and she asked the young man the time, but he didn't answer, only continuing to stare at her. She turned away. At that moment she was hit, and lost consciousness. She came to in a puddle of water behind the block of flats, soaking wet and very cold. She had no idea how long she'd been there. She got up, and, in a state of confusion, leaning on the wall of the block, made her way round to the entrance.

By this time in the morning the Carpați stop was already well frequented and the earlybirds were on their way to work. Victor-Marian Mustață was waiting for his bus and he took cover in the block nearby. He saw a woman's shoe in front of the door, and inside the entrance hall he saw another shoe, plus an umbrella, an open handbag and a big plastic bag with some things in it. He looked in the shrubbery in front of the block and in the ditch from the sewer works, but he couldn't find the victim. He was concerned to get to work on time because he was a station chief for the trolley buses, so he left without enquiring further. Other passersby, for instance Olimpia Alecu and Elena Bădulescu, saw the objects and took no action. Ironically, Sevastița and Vasile Murgu, who lived on Amiciției (Friendship) Street about 30 doors away from Elena, also saw her scattered possessions, while waiting for a bus. Like the others, they simply went on about their business.

Ileana Ionescu, who lived in block 405 where Buluci was attacked, came down to the entrance hall, and turned the lights on. She saw a pair of women's shoes, a lady's umbrella, a black handbag and a plastic bag. When she came out on the pavement of the tram stop, at the end of the block there was another woman she didn't know, who told her about seeing the same objects. Both women went into the entrance hall and looked at the objects and then returned to the tram stop. While they were at the tram stop, Ileana Ionescu saw a young woman walking, leaning on the wall – crawling rather. She came from the end of the block and continued leaning on the wall until she reached the entrance door and went inside. Ionescu did not go to her to see what had happened. Instead she got on the tram and left.

Meanwhile, Elena, leaning on the wall and on the banisters, climbed up to the first floor and knocked on the first door that she saw. When a man, Paraschiv Stoian, came to open it, she asked to come inside to get warm, saying that she was very cold. This was at 4.50 am. He saw a young woman covered in mud and blood. His response was to shut the door in her face. Elena tried another door, where a woman answered, but then shut the door without saying a word.

Elena started crawling back down the stairs, but her strength failed her and she collapsed halfway down. She was found by a woman who asked her what happened, why her feet were bare, and whether the things in the hallway were hers. Elena could only reply that she didn't know. She was obviously wounded and bloody, but, in spite of her appearance, the woman proceeded to lecture her about drinking too much – "are you not ashamed to walk around in such a state?" She put Elena's shoes back on, gave her the bag and handbag, led her to the tram, and metaphorically washed her hands off her.

Elena got back home to Amiciției Street about 6 o'clock. She remembered her umbrella, pink with pink roses, which wasn't handed back to her, and which she never recovered.

Her father, Constantin Ion, called the Militia. The ambulance arrived at about 9 am, nearly 3 hours later, and Elena was admitted to Hospital Nr 9 where she had surgery. The medical-legal investigation report established that "the victim suffered a cranial trauma on the right parietal side, with caving and loss of bone matter on a surface of 3 x 2 cm. The lesion was produced with a hard object requiring 70 – 80 days of medical care."

The two attacks on Margareta Enache and Elena Buluci had taken place within two hours of each other. The first was in Colentina, the far north east of the city, while the second, was a distance away on Calea Griviței in the North East. Interviewed a month later, Elena had no hesitation picking out Rîmaru's photograph from a group of 16. At the time, however, the Militia found it difficult to credit that the same person could have carried out both crimes.

Rîmaru, on the other hand, had no difficulty in recalling both crimes and the circumstances. In a statement, after his arrest, he recounts taking his hatchet, and going out looking for a woman to rape. After attacking Margareta Enache, he continued to be "aroused", and he travelled by bus to the vicinity of the student residence. Then in his frustrated state he walked north west towards Chitila and Pajura. At some point he got on to a bus and saw Elena Buluci. The statement was embellished in the style which became characteristic. As Rîmaru cast around for a defence, he seemed to be inventing responses on the part of the women which would justify the notion that he was provoked -

> "this citizeness who was standing near the sewer works in front of a block of flats asked me what I was looking for there. I answered her that I was looking for a woman in order to sleep with her. She gave me cheek. I got upset and I hit her with the pickaxe (of fire-fighter type) once, I placed her shoes a little to one side, I dragged her behind a block. I tried to rape her but I gave up as some citizens were coming along. I left for the hall of residence where I left the pickaxe and, without sleeping, I rested around one hour, after which I left for the faculty."
> (3rd of June 1971, Militia file 751/B/1971, vol. 4)

Operation Vulturul had been a failure in at least one important aspect. Citizens were not inclined to help secure the public arena. After all, everything about their history was a discouragement. By the start of the 1970s, the Romanians had experienced several major catastrophes at first hand - the financial crash of the 1930s, which had affected a huge proportion of the working and peasant classes, the rise of the Romanian fascists (*Legionari*), which set off the subsequent struggles for power in the mid to late 1930s, World War Two with Romania on the German side in 1941, and then switching sides in 1944, followed by German retaliation and retreat, the Soviet army creating a trail of rape and pillage on its march to Berlin, the rise of the Communist regime, the great postwar famine, and the pain of forced collectivisation.

Added to all this was the sense of being subject to an oppressive and universal surveillance. The presumption was that everyone had something to hide, even when they didn't. Operation Vulturul exposed the yawning gap between high minded rhetoric about citizenship under socialism, and the reality, in which citizens were defenceless against arbitrary arrest and detention. In an environment where the Securitate employed an extensive network of informers, any form of unlicenced public engagement was dangerous, and any unexpected event might be a provocation. The reaction of the average citizen, in these circumstances, was not to play the Good Samaritan. Instead, they tended to cross the street and go on about their own business.

Operation Vulturul was, therefore, unlikely to increase the feeling of public safety. Nevertheless, the efforts of the Militia were about to bear fruit.

Chapter 10

7 May 1971
Iuliana Frunzinschi

Iuliana Frunzinschi was cashier of the food store at 11 Carol Davila Street, sector 6.

This was near the Faculty of Veterinary Medicine where Rîmaru was a student, giving him the opportunity to reconnoitre in advance the closing hour of the store, and the route taken by the cashier to the Central Cashier office, where daily takings were deposited.

At 10 o'clock in the evening hours of the 7th of May, the accounts were completed and the store was closed. Cashier Iuliana Frunzinschi, accompanied by Constanța Petre, who was a salesperson in the same unit, left with the day's takings of 25,687 Lei, to deposit them in the Central Cashier office of 6 Dr Lister Street. It was raining heavily, but it was a short distance, around 300 metres, and they took their usual route, that is through the intersection of Carol Davila and Dr Lister streets.

At the same time, Eugenia Dinicu, a waitress who lived in 22 Dr Lister Street, was making her way home. It was 10.25 pm when she entered the hallway that she walked through in order to reach the basement where she lived. In the dark, she heard a rustle of clothes, but she couldn't see the source, and she hurried into her room. Later on, it was clear that the noise came from Rîmaru, who was hiding in the courtyard to wait for the cashier. There were 10 minutes to the attack.

When Iuliana Frunzinschi and Constanța Petre reached Nr 22 on Dr Lister Street, Ion Rîmaru sprang out of the courtyard, hit cashier Iuliana Frunzinschi on the head with a hatchet, and she fell to the ground. According to Constanța Petre:

"After the first blow, she fell to the ground, I got scared and ran away. When I got off the pavement I turned my eyes and I saw the aggressor leaning over cashier Frunzinschi Iuliana and he continued to hit her. He looked towards me and I saw that he had a fixed, strange gaze."

Eugenia Dinicu, on hearing the noise of a heavy blow on the gate and several moans, came to see what was going on and found the victim in a pool of blood. Meanwhile Constanța Petre ran towards Elefterie Street, where she found Militia platoon leader Iosif Băcilă from the general guard, who she told what had happened, and, returning with him, found Iuliana leaning on the wall, covered in blood, saying – "he took my bag" and "who hit me?".

She had been holding her umbrella in her left hand and the bag of money in her right. Her umbrella had been cut almost in half, and the nail of middle finger had been broken when he wrenched the bag of money out of her hand. Besides the 25,687 Lei of the store's cash she also had in the bag some personal objects, an Electronica transistor radio, a wallet in vinyl of Nile-green colour, a mauve wallet, as well as other small objects of personal use. He had also taken her earrings.

Iuliana was immediately taken and committed to Dr Gheorghe Marinescu Hospital with the diagnosis "recent cranio-cerebral trauma, direct, open".

In his statement Ion Rîmaru says that, immediately after committing this robbery, he threw the bag into the Dâmbovița River, took a *getax* and went to the hall of residence on Mărăști Boulevard where he left the stolen money and the other objects.

By this time, it was late at night, but he did not go to sleep. Instead, he armed himself with his hatchet, and went back to town. At last Operation Vulturul proved an obstacle. Around 4 o'clock in the morning he was stopped and asked for his ID by sergeant major Victor Polojan from the general guard.

Ion Rîmaru pretended to put his hand in his jacket to take out his papers. Instead he took out the hatchet which, under the thick overcoat, would have impeded him as he ran. Then he immediately turned and fled. The militiaman warned him, then fired two shots after him, but he disappeared in the surrounding streets.

Operation Vulturul, at least, had the effect of stepping up surveillance on the streets, but, while the citizens of Bucharest were no more on the alert, Rîmaru's practical difficulties were increasing. There was the matter of clothes. After the first week of May he borrowed light coloured sports jacket from fellow student Florea Fulga, promising to return it the next day. In the morning, Florea Fulga knocked on his locked door. He asked for the jacket, and Rîmaru replied through the closed door that he had forgotten it at the doctor's but that he would recover it. Fulga went again to Rîmaru's room after two hours and asked him to open the door. Besides the existing mess, he saw the jacket soaked in water and put out on a hanger to dry. On the chest there were some big grease stains, or oil stains, in any case it was something that upset him and made him ask what happened to the blouse. Rîmaru did not reply. But he promised that he would clean it by the following day, and if Fulga didn't like it he would reimburse him. The following day, the blouse had been indeed cleaned very well, but it was faded, a fact which made Fulga reject it, taking the money instead. During this period, Rîmaru locked his door with two padlocks, and no one was allowed to enter his room.

The exception was his mother. Ecaterina visited him on the 12th of May. In subsequent interviews with the Militia, she gave different versions of how the money had been discovered. On the first occasion, she even said that Ion had come to Caracal and given it to her. In the next interview, she said that he had given her the money "all of a sudden". Eventually she said that she had gone to Bucharest, as usual on the 12th, and after she received her maintenance money from her husband, she had gone to see Ion. She washed a pullover, several socks and two pairs of underwear, which were bloodstained, and her son told her that he had hit himself with the knife in the stomach to see if he could take it.

"I saw him more agitated than usual. He went out of the room for a moment and, when I looked around the room, I found the pillow, during which time my son entered again and rushed at me. On this occasion,

> when I opened the pillow I saw a wad of money. I
> asked him where he'd got that sum and he said it was
> not my business."
>
> (5th of June 1971, Militia file 751/B/1971, vol. 1)

Ecaterina also noticed a new Electronica transistor radio, newer than the one they had at home. In one more version she said that he told her he had 23,000 Lei and he would be going to Caracal with her when she left. She asked him where the money came from and he told her that he wanted to be rich and he had stalked a cashier, and snatched the money she was carrying. He had also taken a pair of earrings. Ecaterina asked him what he planned to do with the money, and he said he wanted to bury it somewhere. She told him that he should take it home and bury it because, if he was discovered, he could return it.

> "I made an observation to him that he didn't do right,
> and that he was a robber, and he told me that was his
> business and it had nothing to do with me. After this
> discussion, my son Ion asked me if I didn't see how he
> was, that he was changed and that he could not stand
> people."
>
> (2nd of June 1971, Militia file 751/B/1971, vol. 1)

After this discussion with Ion, they went together to the end of bus line Nr 45 where they met his father, Florea Rîmaru. Ion explained to his father how he had acquired the 23,000 Lei, that is he had stolen them from the cashier after hitting her on the head, and he intended to bury it in a forest.

"This discussion took place on the evening of the 12th of May 1971, at the end of bus line Nr 45, Herăstrău Park, being present my wife Rîmaru Ecaterina and my son Rîmaru Ion. He told me that he wanted to bury that money in a forest, without mentioning which forest, so it would not be found by the organs of criminal pursuit, and so that he won't be found as the perpetrator of that fact. He did not tell me which forest he intended to bury the money in. I told him not to bury the money in a forest because somebody else could take them, and that he should go instead to our little house in Caracal and bury it in the storeroom, near the door. He got very angry and struck the wall of the cabin at the end of the line, a blow with his fist."

(2nd of June 1971, Militia file 751/B/1971, vol. 1)

Once the discussion ended, Ion took a *getax* which he paid for himself, and he and Ecaterina went to the hall of residence. Ion took the sum of 23,000 Lei and the earrings which he had hidden in the pillow on his bed from his room. Both the money and the earrings were wrapped in white paper. They then boarded a train at the Gara de Nord and went to Caracal. From the station they went straight to the house in 53 Republicii Boulevard. They placed the money in a sugar tin and buried it in the storeroom near the house. Soon afterwards, after about one hour, Ion returned to Bucharest. The earrings were left with Ecaterina. She took them to Corabia and hid them on the beam of the stable.

"On the 20th of May 1971, I left Bucharest going home to Corabia, boarding the train from Gara de Nord at around 10 am. I reached Corabia and went to my wife's place. I stayed there for the 20th and 21st of May 1971, after which, on the 22nd, I left from Corabia to Caracal to my property there, together with my wife. I asked my wife to show me the place where she had buried the money from the robbery as well as the other objects.

My wife took a shovel and I went with her to our storeroom, where she showed me the place it was buried. It was buried at a distance of circa 50 cm from the threshold of the entrance to the storeroom. I dug very little, around 10 cm, and I found a tin box used as container for sugar, which I took out and opened. On this occasion I saw various sums of money in it. I counted personally each wad of bills and I saw that we were talking about a total of 22,000 Lei. Thus, in one wad there were 92 pieces of 25 Lei each, 54 of 50 Lei each, and 170 pieces of 100 Lei each. They were wrapped in paper and on this paper was noted the number of the pieces in each of them and the respective sum. In the sugar tin, I also saw a wallet in vinyl, of grey or light blue or Nile green colour, which I liked, and also had a mirror inside it. After I saw the money, I took bills from each wad and wrapped them in paper, tearing the old wrapper and throwing it in the cooking machine. I also wrote personally on each packet the respective sums. In addition, my wife showed me a pair of earrings."

(2nd of June 1971, Militia file 751/B/1971, vol. 1)

By this time it is clear that Florea and Ecaterina were primarily concerned with keeping and concealing the money.

"On the morning of the 23rd of May, around 4 am, I left for Bucharest. Before taking over the shift I had a discussion with my son, Rîmaru Ion, with regard to the money he stole from the cashier woman, saying that it would be good to buy a house and not spend it. I happened to know a place close to Herăstrău Park, where there were two houses. When we boarded the bus and got closer to the respective houses, I showed one of them to my son by pointing through the window, advising him to go and see for himself. In this way my son got off the bus, going there. After about one quarter of an hour I found him at the end of Herăstrău Park and he told me he didn't find the address, asking me again where the house was.

Then my son, Rîmaru Ion, showed me the entire route where he went when he robbed the cashier of the sum of 24,000 Lei, where she lived, where the unit she was working was, where the cashiers' office was where she was supposed to deposit the money. He also told me that this cashier was accompanied by another woman whom he supposed also had money on her and he intended to rob her as well but didn't have the time. He fled with the bag and, when he was at a distance from the scene of the attack, he took it to his room in the residence.

Afterwards we went together to a restaurant behind the Operetta where we ate and drank a bottle of beer each. He said that in the meantime he had sold the Electronica transistor radio, which I had seen in his room before leaving for Corabia, for the sum of 160 Lei, to a Gipsy in a market. He told me that he buried in Caracal only 22,000 Lei, and that he had on himself the other 2,000. He gave them to me, together with his identity card, to place them at C.E.C.[9]

After this, we left together going up to Piaţa Dorobanţi where we parted ways. I left for my workplace and he told me he was going to the hall of residence, insisting that I should not expose him."

(2nd of June 1971, Militia file 751/B/1971, vol. 1)

Florea seemed to have some unease about the situation, however, and of the rumours flying around about the latest murder. He had connected it with the hatchet, the knife and Ion's bloody clothes, but, when he confronted Ion about these, the boy denied any involvement. He asked again about Ion's studies, about why he wasn't learning, and then asked whether he wasn't doing things like "those people who committed the deed about which I have heard". Once again Ion denied it. On the other hand, Ion had visited Filareta and reclaimed his hatchet. When Florea asked him why, Ion replied that he "didn't want it to be seen in his father's possession." Florea asked him why he was afraid the hatchet would be found on him, and Ion answered that he'd stolen it from somewhere.

---

9 The only bank to which regular citizens had access.

Chapter 11

Lieutenant Colonel of Militia Ioan Sântea was not pleased to be called away from Arad to review the investigation into the killings in Bucharest. The investigation was already compromised, and he was already deeply suspicious of the Securitate's involvement. There had been a recent murder case in Brașov, which he believed the Securitate had solved by forcing some migrant workers to confess, and, as he suspected, the investigation was hampered by continuous demands for reports coming from the top. Investigators were losing precious time with the paperwork, writing memoranda rather than actually investigating.

There was, however, only one piece of evidence which offered a solution. This was the note which had been found under Mihaela Ursu's body. It was a medical diagnosis sheet on which only the letterhead from the Bucharest Students' Hospital was visible. When Sântea looked at the paper, he realised that there was more information to be gained from it, than was possible at the Centre for Criminology.

By coincidence, his sister worked at the Optics Institute, where they had state of art equipment. He took the note to her, and she managed to establish that they were looking at a sick leave notice from the Students' Hospital, and to decipher two numbers on it – 4 and 6. A team of investigators then trawled through 30,000 medical records in order to match the numbers. In the end, it boiled down to 187 sick leaves corresponding with the number sequence that had been filed, and a further 17 which had not been put on file, so could be considered as lost. One of the 17 names was Ion Rîmaru, a veterinary medicine student.

"On Wednesday the 26th of May current year, I met Rîmaru, and he came to me as usual and gave me his hand to shake as a salutation. When I caught his hand, he gave a start, saying that it hurt him. I asked him what had happened but he made an equivocal gesture without answering."
(Dan Dosinescu, fellow student of Rîmaru's. 2nd of June 1971, Militia file 751/B/1971, vol. 1)

"On the 26th May 1971, the janitor informed me around 8.30 am that the gentleman in room 161 had ruined the table. Around 10.30 am I went to room 161, which was occupied by Rîmaru Ion, and I noticed that the table, in my opinion, was cut with a knife.
I noticed that there was a mess in the room. I opened the window and I found food bits on the window sill, and, to one side, an iron pick, and I threw away both the food and the pick.
The next day at 7.30 am, Rîmaru Ion went to the janitor and asked her if she had gone inside his room because something was missing. She told him I had gone inside and had thrown away that stuff. Then he came to me but found me in a meeting with all the janitor women. He threw me a hostile look as if he would have liked to ask me something. Then he left.
At 9.15 am I met him at the gate and asked him what

he wanted. He told me that he wanted a loudspeaker, and I told him I didn't have one. I asked him why he ruined the table and he replied 'what table, lady (*cucoană*)?' and left."
(Maria Murăruș, administrator at the Nicolae Bălcescu Agronomic Institute. 1st of June 1971, Militia file 751/B/1971, vol. 1)

The Militia actually now had 17 suspects, and they set about making enquiries. Up to 24 hours before the day when they arrested him, however, the investigators were still examining the medical certificate, but it had now become apparent that Rîmaru was the most likely suspect.

At this point, a struggle began between the Militia and the Securitate over responsibility for apprehending the killer. The Militia had done the donkey work, and they resented the Securitate attempt to grab the credit for themselves. At the same time, senior Militia ranks were applying mouth pressure (*mai mult de gura șefilor*) for a politically diplomatic collaboration. The Securitate received the task of coordinating a stakeout operation (*filaj*), while the militiamen and the prosecutors gathered as many clues and witness statements as possible. Ironically, the Militia would have found it easier to stake out Rîmaru's quarters, and as it turned out they would have done a more efficient job.

In fact, the excited Militia officers wanted to initiate the first direct contact with him; and, since all the important actions required advance approval from the superiors running Operation Vulturul, they requested the permission to go ahead. They wanted to approach the student in order to question him, in an apparently amicable and innocent interview, with regard to the medical certificate he had not filed to excuse his absence from classes.

The Militia superiors, however, were sceptical. They believed that the interview would give birth in Rîmaru's mind to the suspicion that he was a murder suspect. Their investigations so far had shown that the student had a withdrawn and impulsive personality, that he habitually carried a knife, and his medical records listed him as suffering from unstable psychopathy. In the circumstances, a violent reaction was more than likely.

On the 27th of May, the day of the arrest, the stakeout was noted in the Securitate officers reports. It was already known that Rîmaru lived alone in a room at a student hall of residence, that his door was permanently locked with two padlocks, that he used to leave the residence every night and return in the morning. The last nail in the coffin was that, surprisingly, they had finally discovered the fact he had been convicted, in the past, of a violent assault for which he had spent five months in prison. Rîmaru was now the number one suspect.

The arrest was programmed to be made at 1 pm. The investigators suspected he would come to the faculty at that time because that was when classes were due to start. In the meantime, the team of Securitate officers stationed themselves outside the hall of residence and watched the building. They were on the alert even though it was believed that he would go straight to the faculty instead of coming back to his lodgings. Each of them had a photograph of Rîmaru, procured by the Militia major Nicolae Ghircoiaș. He had taken it from the baccalaureate diploma, the only photograph that could be found at the time. There was no other more recent photo in the personnel file at the faculty, and it was urgently duplicated and given to the teams of operatives that were looking for him in the city, but at nearly 1 pm Rîmaru had not yet shown himself in the area.

Another team of Militia officers and prosecutors was inside the student hall of residence where Rîmaru lived. They believed that, while he was at the classes, they would have the necessary respite to search the room. The Deputy Chief Prosecutor of Bucharest, Florin Dimitriu, together with Colonel Ion Voicu, from the General Inspectorate of Militia, and the Militia Captain Mihai Irimia constituted the team that entered Rîmaru's room with the help of the residence administrator who opened the door. The time was 11.30 am.

The search revealed the last clues that the prosecutors needed. In Rîmaru's room, the mattress had been stabbed with a knife in numerous places, and the table and the frame of the bed showed traces of blows probably applied with a hatchet. Furthermore, some of the clothes were stained, apparently with blood. There was also a map of the city with several notes, a notebook in which he had recorded, in code, three murders in 1971, together with a list of the objects he had lost at the sites where the murders had taken place, or which he should have taken care not to lose. Among them was the medical certificate.

"This is the man we're looking for," Prosecutor Dimitriu declared emotionally to the other two.

This was on the fourth floor. The prosecutor and the two militiamen were getting ready to finish the search. The door was open, and, at that point they heard the noise of footsteps in the hallway, which seemed to be approaching the room where they were. Someone was coming towards Rîmaru's room, and it wasn't the administrator or the cleaning lady, but Rîmaru himself, irritated because the door of his room was open, and ready to demand explanations from the intruders. The surprise was total, for both parties.

Rîmaru discovered that there were some men who looked suspicious in his room, probably militiamen or Securitate, or at least they looked like it. The team inside the room were amazed to see on the threshold a young man who seemed to be their suspect, who they certainly had not expected to have evaded the stakeout teams posted at the entrance of the building.

How did this first meeting between pursued and pursuers go? The magazine of the Ministry of the Interior later published a detailed account.

> "Presence of mind on the part of Colonel Voicu Ion. He had heard footsteps in the corridor. He gave a start. He saw Rîmaru appear in the frame of the door. A second (how long a second is) passed, in which the suspect's known characteristics are mentally compared with those of the man in the door.
> 'How are you, Ionel my boy (*măi, Ionele*), cheers!' says Colonel Voicu, offering him his hand.
> In a reflex gesture, Rîmaru offers his own hand. The colonel grabs it firmly, preventing from that very moment whatever might have happened.
> 'What are you looking for in here?' Rîmaru asked angrily.
> 'I am the deputy chief prosecutor of the Capital and

we want to sit and talk to you,' Dimitriu replied, showing the suspect his warrant card.

During this time, Captain Irimia had already gone behind Rîmaru, in the hallway, in order to block his way in case he ran.

'I am not talking except outside,' Rîmaru replied, trying to free himself from the hands of Colonel Voicu and Captain Irimia, who had now grabbed him as well.

'Calm down and show a proper attitude!' the prosecutor said, drawing his attention to the warrant card again. Rîmaru continued to try to free his hands. The prosecutor now also grabbed him by the hand Colonel Voicu held, and they pulled him into the room.

'Let go of my left arm and then we talk!'

Pulling away, the suspect struggled, biting Captain Irimia by the hand, without succeeding in freeing himself.

'You let go of the bag,' they shouted at him.

Under his right arm he had a tight hold on a black vinyl bag with handles which were hung around his shoulder. For minutes in a row, there were efforts being made on one side and on the other. Eventually, they immobilised him and pulled the bag away. In it were the hatchet and the knife wrapped in a red towel."

(*Pentru Patrie*[10], Nr 11 / 1972)

Of course, there was a certain satisfaction about the Militia's awareness that Rîmaru had managed to pass the

---

10 For Our Homeland.

entire Securitate cordon, and barge in on the people in the room. The fact was, it seemed, Rîmaru used the back door rather than the main entrance; not in order to hide himself but because that was his usual practice.

Officially, an acceptable explanation was found in order to save face for the Securitate officers. The photograph was old, and Rîmaru's appearance was different from that in the photo. This allowed him to pass unobserved by one of the teams posted at the main entrance of the building. Unofficially, the militiamen knew that the Securitate had staked out only one of the entrances, and forgotten about the other.

Part 4

Chapter 12

The Investigation

In the courtyard of Militia Headquarters in Bucharest, Rîmaru was dragged out of the car in which he had been transported. It was a violent struggle, because he was still trying to resist arrest. Ioan Sântea, the Militia officer from Arad, who recently had joined the investigation team, happened to enter the inner yard at the same time, and was impressed by the vigour with which Rîmaru tried to free himself from the militiamen. The officers, themselves, could barely manage to contain his wild plunging as they tugged him into the building. When he reached the office, however, Rîmaru's body drooped, his energies exhausted, like a "wild beast" who understood that it had lost the fight.

On the second day of his arrest, the 28th of May, Rîmaru was shown the arrest warrant. He remained in preventative detention until the finalising of the investigation and his presentation in court. The prosecutors only opened the file, Nr 751/B/1971, detailing his pursuit and detention, on the 2nd of June. Up to that time, there had been various other intermediary stages, such as a medical analysis of his blood type and dental imprint. In addition, there were several initial discussions, testing the ground between him and the investigators.

In those days, an arrest warrant and criminal arrest in

Romania could imply torture, or moderate beatings. The prisoner could also be subject to routine derision and abuse. The Militia considered these methods as normal practice. Prisoners of the Securitate, on the other hand, were subject to harsher regimes, especially in the previous decade.

Militiamen used to amuse themselves, also, by making detainees do things which appeared simple, but in reality were almost impossible. For example, the picture of Nicolae Ceaușescu was a feature of every room in each state institution, and a prisoner would be ordered to hold it against the wall – by his nose alone. The picture was large, with a heavy wooden frame, and the tip of your nose would slide on the glass, which meant that you dropped the picture of comrade General Secretary, you bandit, how could you dare commit such an offence? Then the good cop would leave the room, to be replaced by the bad cop, who took care to restore the honour of the Militia, with a good beating. Another strategy for amusement was to use a police dog to guard the prisoner who was made to stand balancing on one leg. If he let the other leg touch the floor, the dog was trained to growl and bark, as if about to jump at the victim and tear him to pieces.

There is no proof, however, that Rîmaru was subject to ill treatment. It is likely that he might have been hit, in the initial stage of the investigation, more precisely when he had been just brought in. In a recent interview, when asked about this topic, Colonel Sântea refused to admit directly that violence was used to restrain, coerce or make Rîmaru confess, merely remarking, "You understand our attitude, it was about our families". On the other hand, it is clear that violence directed at the prisoner would have been an exception, rather than a practice that lasted for the entire investigation.

The explanation may be that Rîmaru was now an exceptional prize. One day after the arrest, Nicolae Ceauşescu was due to return from his triumphant journey to the capital of North Korea. Such a high profile case would be the subject of attention all over the world, the investigators assumed, and the suspect had to be treated with every formality, if only to demonstrate that socialist justice respected the law and the rights of the suspect.

The single article on Rîmaru which appeared in the communist press, the one in *Pentru Patrie* magazine, made a point of highlighting the fact that Rîmaru had received an impeccable arrest and detention.

"Rîmaru had arrived at the Militia with certain preconceived ideas. He expected brutal behaviour and he found himself treated in a way that was more than polite (especially towards such a man as he knew himself to be). He saw that the diet corresponded to the gastritis he suffered from. He always had access to a doctor, when he wanted one. Those guarding him were also very correct in their behaviour. He finally understood that the investigators meant only to establish the truth, that it was the law which would decide his fate; because, as a result of his mistaken notions, he had asked if he would stand trial, and if he would be able to bring a defence counsel. He asked for a lawyer and one was brought to him, even in that stage of the investigation. All these requests of his were satisfied, respecting the precise requirements of the laws of our country."
(*Pentru Patrie*, Nr 12 / 1972)

For Romanians the subtext of the lines above was clear. Rîmaru believed he would be tortured, but we, the Militia, didn't do it. He believed we would assassinate him, and declare he committed suicide, or that he tried to run away, but we didn't do it. Also, he believed that, if he escaped the investigation alive, the trial would be a sham, just a simple formality. We didn't do that either, *although he would have deserved it fully*.

On the other hand, when the investigators realised that Rîmaru was lacking in education and had a very weak intellectual capacity, he also became a curiosity for them. It was the first time they had faced a killer of his kind. He was unique, and deserved to be studied, which, in some sense, actually happened. His gestures and reactions stayed in the memory of the investigators for many years afterwards.

The investigation teams and specialists, who had the task of setting in motion the formalities of arrest and identification, were impatient to get started.

Leading the teams of investigators and prosecutors involved in the interrogation were Chief Prosecutor of the Capital Dumitru Popescu, Deputy Chief Prosecutor Florin Dimitriu, and Office Chief Prosecutor Vasile Comşa, together with the militiamen Lieutenant Colonel Ioan Sântea, Major Nicolae Ghircoiaş, and Captain Ion Voicu.

They already had the necessary evidence. The dental imprint was identical to those on the bodies of the victims. So was the blood type A2. There were deposits of human blood on various clothes taken from the hall of residence, and the watch he had on his wrist belonged to Gheorghiţa Popa. Everything pointed to the conclusion that Rîmaru was a psychopath, and the burden of proof had already been resolved. They now had the urgent task of finding out whether he had been responsible for various other unsolved crimes. It would be more useful if he incriminated himself, so the investigators decided on an unusual strategy.

The interrogation would take the form of relaxed conversations. They would be so relaxed that they wouldn't necessarily touch on the crimes of which he was suspected. At the same time, the team would use the usual strategy of placing him in a cell with a Militia under-officer, disguised as a thief, who would make friends with him and obtain as much information as possible.

They began by asking Rîmaru about his family, about his life as a student, about his travels, about how he spent his free time and about the state of his health. In reply, he kept silent or answered in monosyllables, with long pauses. Later on, he made the first statement in which there were general references to his lifestyle.

They now had enough information to summon his father, which they did on the evening of the 27th of May, hours after the arrest. It was a tense confrontation in the presence of the investigators. When his father was led in, Rîmaru merely looked at him – "an ugly look", at which Florea cried out, "How should I know what you did? ...How?"

Florea continued by reproaching Ion. If he had got himself arrested, he certainly must have done something, and, if so, he should confess, so that he could help. After the meeting, it was Florea's turn to be questioned, at which point the subject of the money stolen from the cashier appeared. Until that moment, the Militia did not know a thing about the involvement of his parents in covering up the evidence of his crimes. Over the next two days they extracted as much information as possible about Florea and his relationship with Ion, drawing up a detailed outline of family life and the influence of his parents.

Florea Rîmaru was a violent individual, a wifebeater, who had given up married life and moved to Bucharest to live with Filareta Călin, a weaver in a state enterprise. He had no responsibilities, he did not take part financially in any way, not even for food, although his income was considerable for the time, some 4,000 Lei[11]. He was a driver working on the night buses. Buses in which his son used to travel until the morning, and which were his favourite places for selecting his victims. But that was not all. Ionel just liked to travel by bus and would often sit there dreaming until the bus was at the end of the line. At other times, on the way home, father and son would meet, travelling together in the deserted city. Florea never questioned him about what he was looking for at such a late hour. At the wheel, to make time pass, he would tell his son about life and women. Grasping his hatchet in his fist under his jacket, Ion listened.

The investigators also heard that Florea knew about the attack on cashier Iuliana Frunzinschi on the 7th of May 1971, and about where the money was buried in Caracal. They learnt that Ion washed his bloody clothes at Filareta Călin's house. According to Florea, he had kept Ion's favourite weapons, the hatchet and the knife, so that he would not do anything stupid. He suspected Ionel of bad deeds, but didn't think he was the serial killer who frightened the city. This horrible thought hadn't occurred to him, even when, during Operation Vulturul, he had taken part in the meeting with

---

11 Two average salaries at the time.

the bus drivers of Bucharest, who had been asked to call the Militia every time they saw a passenger with clothes stained with blood or mud.

Nevertheless, Florea Rîmaru could not be arrested. There was no proof that he took part in the crimes. He was not the murderer. The investigators, after listening to him, could not do anything but reproach him for being violent with his wife and children, for entering into a pact with the murderer the moment he found out about the robbery of the cashier, and for being morally culpable because he did not have the strength of character to denounce him immediately.

Once the investigators had a fuller picture however, they initiated a frantic questioning of Ion's family and friends, together with searches of every address he was known to frequent.

The first reaction of Ion's parents was to panic. They had good reason. Both of them were involved in hiding money and weapons for Ion, and both of them must have had strong suspicions about what he was doing. Ecaterina, in particular, was in a frantic state. When her home in Corabia was searched the day after Ion's arrest, she went straight to Bucharest. In a statement made on the 1st of June, she describes her hysteria.

"From the train station I went straight to ITB Floreasca Garage where my husband works, and there I found that he was at the Militia station but they didn't know which one, and I stayed there all morning at the garage, after which I went to my son's faculty hall of residence but they told me I couldn't go in because he was with the Militia, and, after I stayed there for a while, I returned to the garage where I learned that my husband hadn't come back. And, in this situation, I went to his home in Colentina, but I didn't find anyone there and, after waiting about half an hour, when I wanted to leave, my husband was just arriving. We did not stay together at his house at all and we both went to the bus station, following which I intended to return to the train station. On the road I asked him what Ion did, to which he replied that our son was arrested, that he had been arrested as well. He told me that it could be about some money and then he said the Militia supposed Ion could have committed murders but that he didn't believe it. I said to my husband that I didn't know Ion when I saw him last, having a changed expression. I reproached him at the same time that he should have taken care of him. My husband said that he advised Ion not to go on missing from the residence during the nights. I don't know how my husband knows about this aspect with missing from the residence during the nights, as he did not tell me."

(1st of June 1971, Militia file 751/B/1971, vol. 1)

The house in Corabia had already been searched, but the knife she'd taken from Ion was actually hidden in Caracal, along with the proceeds of the robberies. On the evening of the 30th of May, she was told to present herself to the Militia on the next day. Imagining that there would be another search, she travelled to Caracal at 8 o'clock that night, found a more secure hiding place for the knife, and travelled back to Corabia at 6 am to present herself to the Militia.

Florea had been equally busy. On being summoned by the Militia on the 27th, he had met Iona Daju, a conductor at the same garage, and given her Ion's ID card and the sum of 1,900 Lei. He met her on the way back to the garage on the 29th, and now she insisted on returning them.

Back at the garage Ecaterina was waiting. He told her that he had been questioned by the Militia for 24 hours, and they talked about the searches, at which point Ecaterina asked why the Militia had also searched her house. Florea replied, "what, don't you know that Ion stole the money hitting a woman on the head?". He also instructed her, when she got back to Corabia, to burn the papers on which he'd written the sums, and in which he had wrapped the money, along with the vinyl wallet. About 6 pm they were joined by Filareta Călin, and they went back to her house in Simetriei Street, where they discussed the blood on some of Rîmaru's clothes, and his recent despair. For some reason, Ecaterina later denied that the visit took place. She did, however, go to their house in Caracal, and burn the wrappers and the wallet. She left the money where it was.

On the 31st of May 1971, a search was conducted at the Rîmaru family house in Caracal, 53 Republicii Boulevard, and a metallic box was found buried in the storeroom in front of the house, in which there were a number of banknotes of 100, 50, and 25 Lei, in total the sum of 22,000 Lei. Also found, was a pair of earrings belonging to Iuliana Frunzinschi, which the mother had received from her son, Ion Rîmaru, admitting that they came from the theft.

Another search at Filareta Călin's house at 15C Simetriei Street turned up the rest of the money, namely 1,000 Lei, hidden in a pillow, and 275 Lei were found on Florea, as well as the identity card of his son Ion Rîmaru. The sum of 1,275 Lei and the identity card were collected in the course of the investigation. On being questioned about the money, Ion admitted that he did indeed hide in Caracal only the sum that was found, 22,000 Lei, and that, besides this, he had given his father 2,000 Lei from the stolen sum. He had spent the difference buying various items of clothing. He also gave his mother the earrings as a present, and the transistor radio had been sold to an unknown person on Calea Victoriei.

The searches went on. Rîmaru's student room was searched on the day of his arrest and again on the 31st of May. The searchers picked up, among other objects: one men's coat of navy blue colour and a men's jacket in brown and yellow checks, used. Also collected was the receipt Nr 2520 of the 17th of May 1971, in the fictitious name Florea Vrănescu of Bucharest, 64 Mărăști Boulevard, issued by the *Nufărul* enterprise. The receipt was for a striped men's suit in semi-terylene, colour navy-Nile green.

Later on, in statements made on the 7th and the 16th of June 1971, Rîmaru admitted that the men's jacket in brown and yellow checks, the men's coat in navy fabric, and the striped men's suit in semi-terylene, colour navy-Nile green, were stolen on the night of 19/20 July 1970 from the display window of the Confecția store in 385-387 Calea Rahovei.

The interrogation was now in full swing. The initial days in which Rîmaru was uncommunicative, or restricted himself to precise answers, were over. So were the nights of probing, where they provoked him to open up. Real conversations focused on the state of his health, because Rîmaru preferred this subject to any other, and he would declare that he was feeling ill or not very well. After several days, he started to talk, without offering details, about his nocturnal travels, on the streets and on the buses, when he would meet women to whom he proposed sexual relations, and, on being refused, he would strike them.

Patiently, the investigators waited for a suitable moment to suggest more detail, how he did it, what he said, how he hit them. Finally, as the days passed, Rîmaru admitted murder after murder, rape after rape. He admitted to all the crimes for which he was tried. Sometimes, as if he were now a different person, he insisted vehemently, when one of his interrogators appeared dubious, with more details about the deed, in order to demonstrate his own guilt.

It was not a complex interrogation. Rîmaru was not clever enough to play games with the interrogators, and the evidence was irrefutable. The style of the investigation was, however, very different to the usual practice of the militiamen and prosecutors.

Rîmaru had sleeping and waking patterns to which the militiamen were not accustomed. While they consumed countless coffees and packs of cigarettes in order to keep awake during the long nights of investigation, Rîmaru was sleepy during the day and wide awake at the night. He had, after all, been wandering the streets of the city at this time for more than a year. The investigation continued at night, because it was the most suitable time. At 5 in the morning, everybody, except him, was exhausted. Two hours later, when they were trying to send him back to be locked up, Rîmaru asked the investigators to stay. He had something else to say. They stayed. During the day, Rîmaru was not disposed to talk, and the prosecutors did not interrupt his rhythm because they realised it would be a mistake. In the end they decided that in the morning, at the end of the interrogation, other teams would take over the statements to compare them with the previous ones, to explore misleading trends in the records – in short – to prepare for the next night of interrogation.

The team of investigators had no doubt about Rîmaru's guilt. On the other hand, it presented them with a dilemma. Rîmaru had to die. No question. The law, however, stipulated that, in a case where the accused had no awareness, and the crimes were committed in an unconscious state, he could not be executed. He had to be condemned to detention in a specialised clinic.

This was a result that would be unacceptable to the investigators, to the locals of Bucharest, and to the leaders of the Communist Party. Yes, Rîmaru was mad, but not so mad as to lack awareness about the consequences of his actions.

So, this was the question the team was working towards. Was Rîmaru responsible for his actions? To put it another way: was Rîmaru a person with significant psychological damage? Did this damage, if it existed, excuse him of responsibility for his actions?

The prosecutors needed an opinion about this question, but answering it was not their responsibility. For this, it was necessary to refer to a committee of psychiatric expertise that had been assembled from the very beginning of the interrogation.

Chapter 13

Six doctors were invited to be part of the Committee of Psychiatric Expertise which was to decide on Rîmaru's responsibility for his crimes. They were psychiatrists Professor Dr Vasile Predescu, Dr Virgil Angheluță, Dr Tiberiu Vlad, and Dr Elena Vrabie. These were joined by pathologist Dr Adriana Manolescu and Professor Dr Vlad Voiculescu from the Neurology Institute. These were the leading authorities in the country, and they had a network of assistants at their disposal.

The Militia Captain Cornel Leuce was sent to various sites in the country in order to trace the Rîmaru genealogy. One of the doctors, accompanied by a nurse, did a social investigation in the towns of Caracal and Corabia, interviewing Rîmaru's teachers, former colleagues and neighbours. The committee also had access to Rîmaru from the first stages of the investigation, checked him repeatedly during the interrogation, and kept him under surveillance.

All this was because the doctors had to supply an authoritative opinion. First of all, it had to be established whether Rîmaru was suffering from a psychiatric illness capable of affecting his *discernământ* (ability to discriminate). Secondly, whether any psychiatric illness that they might discover was affecting his general consciousness. Thirdly, whether, in the moment of attack, Rîmaru was in a state of total or partial unconsciousness. Finally, they had to decide whether medical strategies were appropriate, and, in that case, what strategies they should recommend.

The conclusions of the doctors were published several months later in *Pentru Patrie* magazine. As the title suggests, *Pentru Patrie* was licensed to publish the official view of such important issues. From its point of view, the doctors' role was to reassure its public that everything had been done to justify Rîmaru's execution.

Crucially, the doctors use terms and concepts unfamiliar outside of their own country. After all none of them could go to international conferences, or communicate with professionals abroad. In addition, their view of society was constrained by the ideology of the Party. Within the framework of the Party, society was bound together by a variety of collectives, which were supposed to nourish and discipline individual members. In the case of Rîmaru, the doctors were now supposed to explain how his behaviour had escaped correction, while, at the same time, taking care not to suggest that the kind of lunacy, which was a feature of decadent capitalism, could also exist in a socialist society.

In an interview with the Committee a number of issues were addressed. First was the influence of Rîmaru's childhood and early conditioning. Professor Predescu, the most senior member of the group, ran through what was known about Rîmaru's upbringing – his dysfunctional parenting, his outbursts at school, his delinquency, and came to the conclusion that he lacked the capacity to adapt to social conventions and requirements. "This development is what we consider as pathological and call it an aberrant development of personality."

On the other hand the panel had to consider Rîmaru

responsible because psychiatric illnesses

> "...have different degrees, manifest with different
> intensities. We considered Rîmaru responsible for his
> deeds because, from the point of view of his disorders,
> he never was entered in the category of those with
> disorders of psychotic intensity, with delirium, with
> hallucinations, who act with no motivation of any
> kind."
> (*Pentru Patrie*, Nr 11 / 1972)

Next, Professor Voiculescu took up the issue of Rîmaru's
"periodic epilepsy", which had been diagnosed in March.
Looking at encephalograms, he was unable to see evidence
of an epileptic state. In any case, he says, to be excused
responsibility, an epileptic must show that, in the moment
of committing the crime, he was suffering from an
"abnormal disorder of consciousness". Meaning that, even
with manifestly mentally ill people, the crucial problem,
from a judicial point of view, was the question: did he have
an awareness (*discernământ*) of the act? In Rîmaru's case, he
was always aware that he was doing something punishable
by law.

This led the team to the next important question. Given that
Rîmaru was an "abnormal person", why was he responsible
for his crimes? Dr Vlad had two main answers. First, was
the fact that he set off with the intention of robbery or rape.
He was going to work, and he reached finality, depending
on his achievement. The second point was that he was not
driven by an irresistible impulse. He cultivated weapons for
the purpose, showing that he acted with consciousness of

what he was going to do. Furthermore, his impulses were not uncontrollable, because Rîmaru made several attempts which were interrupted when he heard footsteps or he saw a light being switched on. So he was in a state of total vigilance and he had an absolute instinct for self preservation. This was not the behaviour of a person who is really mentally ill.

> "The abnormal is the man who has possibilities but has no scruples. But, I repeat, has possibilities. We do not contest Rîmaru's abnormality. But the abnormal person is responsible for his deeds."
> (*Pentru Patrie*, Nr 11 / 1972)

Professor Predescu added at this moment that it was not only heredity but also environment which was responsible for the "aberrant personality". In the case of Rîmaru, the father's treatment of his family encouraged the "pathological traits of development" to grow.

Dr Angheluță now raised the question of the social (and socialist) environment, using language more appropriate for a Party functionary than a medical man, and reminding the panel about the problem of ideology and the collective responsibility.

Rîmaru had been developing over a long period of time, so how was it possible that no one noticed, he asked.

> "Rîmaru was leaving for the night, he came back in the morning exhausted, he locked himself in the room, he did not attend classes... But he was nevertheless living within a collective. Didn't the collective have

the duty to inform about of these aspects?"
(*Pentru Patrie*, Nr 11 / 1972)

He followed this by arguing Rîmaru's education should
be a warning to the pedagogues about paying attention to
problem families.

> "With Rîmaru, I think this attention was of a very
> weak quality. There are things that impress even a
> beginner, it is not mandatory to be a great specialist.
> There existed in that place a disciplinary council, there
> was the rector's office, there were people meant to
> follow the students' activity. I asked myself: how did it
> happen that nobody knew? All his colleagues avoided
> coming into contact with him, nobody wanted to sleep
> in the same room with Rîmaru. Nobody asked the
> question: why? This is a problem to which I cannot
> give an answer."
> (*Pentru Patrie*, Nr 11 / 1972)

The implication was that the structures didn't work,
and in a sense this was a kind of bombshell for the other
experts. It's not clear whether Angheluță was trying to shift
responsibility, and in which direction, but his use of the
phrase "it is not mandatory to be a great specialist", seems
to be aimed at his fellow panelists.

Professor Predescu tried to defuse the challenge by
suggesting that Rîmaru was such a dangerous psychopath
that he cast a shadow over his colleagues, even at the
university, thus crippling the efforts of the collective.

"This element was preformed and was a consequence of a development of the kind I tried to expound. Of course social measures cannot liquidate psychopathy… But they can shape it, thus devoiding it of the criminal consequences that constitute a traumatising concern for a very large collective of people."
(*Pentru Patrie,* Nr 11 / 1972)

Dr Vrabie addressed the issue of how much Rîmaru had been dissimulating as they examined him. As she saw it, the habit of dissimulation was part of his personality, something which pre-dated his criminal activities. This was one the "traits of psychopathy", and she had noticed it in the first clinical observations. His use of doctors, for example, was always connected to his crimes. The day after an assault he would visit a doctor, "always creating a sort of alibi in order to cover himself in case he would be identified."

At first he would fake falling, when asked to make a statement, but he did it in such a way as to avoid hurting himself. "He picked himself up from the floor, after he mimed a fit, and we told him: 'Come on, Ion, quit playing the fool and say the truth!' And he gave the first statement: 'Yes, it was me.'"

Professor Voiculescu added a comment about Rîmaru's language. "He used few words but even here there was an element of deception. Talking about the Gara de Nord and the statue in front of it, he called it 'the iron man'. To which Professor Predescu drew his attention: 'Listen, you, stop… like you don't know…!' And he started laughing and admitted."

His use of *discernământ* and dissimulation were, therefore, extremely acute, and this was the essential element of responsibility.

Professor Predescu summed up by arguing that Rîmaru was calculatedly playing the simpleton. At certain times he appeared not to know what a knife or a plate was. But his performance was undermined on many occasions. Sometimes, he would write correctly, then cross out what he had done and repeat it in the wrong form. There were multiple examples of this, but, when he saw that dementia wasn't working, he started telling the Professor that he heard voices which gave him specific orders. According to Predescu, however, this was never a characteristic of the "truly psychotic". It merely proved his ability to consciously follow a certain goal. Unlike a psychotically ill person he could reproduce from memory, coherently, in sequence, the deeds he had committed.

> "It was precisely deduced that he made a connection between the instruments of the crime which he was shown and his own actions. This was further proof that he was fully lucid while these actions were going on. His actions happened with such lucidity that any oversight was noted in his personal notebook, as also noted were the order of the victims, the place where he committed the deed, what he forgot there... So, even in the most intense moment of the criminal deeds, he had perfect lucidity, he was left with the memory and took measures to avoid discovery."
> (*Pentru Patrie*, Nr 11 / 1972)

Dr Angheluță concluded by saying that they had

interpreted Rîmaru's state of mind "from our point of view", and concluded that Rîmaru was responsible for his actions. His punishment was the responsibility of the law.

The Committee had done its job, with one notable codicil. As Professor Predescu and Dr Vlad pointed out none of this could be laid at the door of the medical profession. The deficiencies were rather, to be found in the "organisational-administrative and educational-social" framework in "various institutions and collectives through which he had passed and spent his life."

There was now no barrier to Rîmaru's conviction. He had initially spoken freely, admitting the crimes with which he was charged. When he read the report of the Committee, he recanted, saying that he did not admit to anything he had said until then. After this he was silent.

Part 5

Chapter 14

The Trial

The Romanian justice system adopted the Napoleonic Code during the 19th century, and in 1971, their trial procedure differed significantly from that of English or American courts. There was no appeal to precedent, for example, and the entire proceedings were less adversarial. Finally, instead of a jury, the case was heard by a panel of judges and "people's assessors".

The process of investigation, therefore, was a fundamental part of the trial. In Rîmaru's case the process lasted for two months. The statements of the accused, the witness statements, and those of the victims who survived were matched against each other. The physical evidence was catalogued and compared with the statements. Finally, the survivors were called in for an identification parade. Rîmaru faced them, shackled and with the gaze of a vanquished animal, but he was capable of provoking terror. Seeing him, they trembled.

The investigation and the subsequent indictment were completed on the 26th of July. The week before that, the material was presented to Rîmaru. He read the entire file in a loud, slow voice, sometimes reading the same page two or three times.

It took another week for the prosecutors Dumitru

Popescu, Florin Dimitriu and Vasile Comşa to put together the bill of indictment (*rechizitoriu*). Then, the file was sent to the Deputy Prosecutor General for confirmation. Two days later, on the 28th of July, the file was confirmed and approved. Next, the file was forwarded to the Tribunal of the Municipality of Bucharest, which had been chosen as the appropriate court. Placed on the judges' table, the file received a new registration number, from the tribunal list: 3900/1971.

In those days the Bucharest Tribunal was housed in a smaller building near the imposing Palace of Justice. When the Rîmaru trial started, the president of the panel of judges was the president of the tribunal, magistrate Ion Manole. He was joined on the panel by fellow judge Theodor Cîmpeanu, and three people's assessors. The public prosecutor was Nicolae Butnaru.

Rîmaru's trial started on the 1st of September 1971 and took place in special conditions, for a number of reasons. Now that the killer had a face and a name, and was in custody, there had been a cautious press coverage, with photographs and details from the victims' stories. First of all, it was considered that the accused needed increased protection. The locals of Bucharest, some of them revolted, some of them just curious, wanted to see him, in great numbers. The Militia and the Securitate had intelligence reports warning there were people disposed to lynch him if they had the chance. Rîmaru was placed under special guard, and the itinerary by which he was brought to the tribunal altered each day.

In any case there were, around the tribunal building, thousands and thousands of locals who wanted to take part in the hearings. As a result, the tribunal decided that participation in the trial could take place only by official invitation.

The hall was full to its limits. The invited audience, dressed as for a special occasion, occupied the chairs on both sides of the room. Aside from the prosecutors, the majority were Militia and Securitate personnel. Alongside them, were representatives of various party organisations from the city.

Rîmaru entered the courtroom accompanied by four militiamen, handcuffed on either side to one of his escorts. They instructed him on what movements to make: when to stand, when to sit, where to sit. His lawyer asked the court's permission to take off the handcuffs, at least for the time that he would be questioned, but the request was denied, on the grounds of security.

He was dressed in a new penitentiary uniform, with a white shirt underneath, and his appearance created a hubbub. At first sight he seemed resigned to his situation, his expression vacant and distracted. In front of him there was a microphone, which he alone used when he stood to reply to the questions. From time to time, he looked at the public, smiling gently.

In particular, his eyes dwelt on the victims who had survived and whose state of health allowed them to be present in the hall. During the proceedings, Iuliana Frunzinschi, the cashier, fainted and had to leave the hall, due to Rîmaru's "animal gaze".

The proceedings began with a motion from Mihail Ghiga, court appointed lawyer for the defence. He requested a new expert committee to check the results of the first body of experts, on the basis that Rîmaru could not be deemed to be fully responsible for his actions, since a normal man would not commit such crimes. The request was denied by the tribunal, since the first committee's report was the well documented result of repeated examinations.

Ghiga's next strategy was to request the court to show clemency. In the first instance, because the accused was "abnormal". In the second, because the intention of the assaults was rape, rather than murder. So, Ghiga argued, the court should not choose the death penalty. Instead, the penalty should be a term in prison, changing the charge from highly aggravated murder, to one of premeditated murder.

In reply, the prosecution presented a witness who declared that she recognised in the dock the young man who, on the morning of the 9th of May 1970, had passed on that street, and asked the gathered people if something had happened in that courtyard. This was after Elena Oprea, the first victim, had been transported to the hospital in a critical condition. If Rîmaru had enquired after result of his action, he would have found out that he had endangered a life. The murderer knew the deadly result of his first aggression. So Ghiga's arguments fell one by one, and as the lawyer himself commented some months later his arguments had a pretty low prospect of success:

> "The notion of attenuated responsibility is not inscribed in our penal law. In other countries also, justice does not recognise anything other than the two extreme situations. The subject of the crime acted with *discernământ* and is thus responsible, or is lacking *discernământ* and thus without responsibility.

Besides these, the deeds existed as fundamental aspects, as well as Rîmaru's trial-related attitudes. We could observe Rîmaru adopting some attitudes which were completely in conformity with his interests. For instance, attempting, in his last address in the trial, to pass a part of the guilt on his father; simulating a fall during my pleading, precisely when I was maintaining the thesis of attenuated responsibility; writing a plea in which he narrated his deeds, but in which he passes over the most savage murders, maintaining he was hallucinating. He also attempted to change his appearance, growing a moustache in prison, so that at the appeal he maintained that it was possible that part of the crimes might have been committed by another student who looked like him.

All this tended to convince the judges that Rîmaru was not lacking in intelligence and was well oriented towards his goals. I myself could not afford to draw unfavourable conclusions to the theses I was obliged to support. But, if I had believed that the decision taken was unjust, I would have considered it my duty to make use of all legal routes in order to remove what I would have seen as an injustice."

(*Pentru Patrie*, Nr 1 / 1973)

Rîmaru himself had forgotten the pretences he had adopted during the investigation in front of the prosecutors and militiamen, and, for the period of the trial, he appeared to be logical when he answered questions, describing the cases of murder and rape and offering further details to those uncovered by the investigation.

In his final address, Rîmaru made new, surprising statements, maintaining that his father had participated in some of his crimes. Trying to construct his father's guilt, Rîmaru described how he urged him to rob and rape the women, to act during rainfall or use a car so that his tracks would not be followed by police dogs. In his youth, Rîmaru said, his father did the same things, and had not been apprehended to this day.

To make matters even more complicated, one of the victims, Maria Iordache, declared, during the trial, that it had been not Ion Rîmaru who attacked her, but his father. Florea Rîmaru behaved badly to his family, he supported his son by hiding his money and taking his bloodstained clothes to the cleaners, so the court decided his complicity was possible and ordered the arrest of the father, during the trial itself. In an instant, Florea Rîmaru was being arrested by two officers dressed in plain clothes, to the wild applause of the public.

As it turned out there was no evidence to support the arrest, and Florea was freed later on. In the appeal addressed to the Supreme Tribunal, Rîmaru withdrew his previous accusations and affirmed that his father was, in fact, innocent. "I said that about him in the tribunal, I don't know why, probably due to pain because he beat mother up when he came home...".

There was, therefore, no evidence of complicity in the commission of the attacks. For his complicity in concealing evidence, Florea went unpunished by the law, given his relationship to the killer.

Prosecutor Nicolae Butnariu, the accuser, was also applauded in court. He developed each individual case and underlined Rîmaru's evil effect on society and his fellow citizens. He talked about his necrophiliac tendencies, his habit of consummating the sexual act even after the victims' spasms of agony ended, about his aggressiveness that continued even after the death of the victims, about his pleasure in biting the vagina and breasts of the victims, ripping off pieces of flesh that were not even found at the crime scene, or about the vampirism he showed in sucking the victims' blood.

He requested, at the same time - alongside Rîmaru's defence lawyer who had asked for acquittal - the withdrawal of a charge of attempted rape which had been introduced by the prosecution. This was the case of Stana Sărăcin, from 1/2 May 1971. The court decided to send the case to the prosecutors' office in order to establish the real criminal.

In the evening of the 3rd of September 1971, at the end of the trial that lasted three days, the court prepared to withdraw for deliberation. The prosecution, through prosecutor Butnariu, was asking for capital punishment in the name of the law. The defence, through lawyer Ghiga, was asking, in the name of humanity, committal to prison.

The court found that, since Rîmaru did not care about humanity, the force of the law demanded full satisfaction. Judge Ion Manole took into consideration the fact that Rîmaru had already been condemned to five months for robbery, and the fact that he was on trial for highly aggravated offences:

"... which, through their perilous nature, roused the public's indignation profoundly and created a state of fear and insecurity among salaried women who were

161

obliged, by the nature of their work, to circulate at late hours; that, although he had all the conditions to develop normally and progress in learning, even becoming a student, he preferred to abandon learning and give himself to actions of rarely met ferocity."
(File Nr 3900/1971 of the Tribunal of the Municipality of Bucharest)

In fact, Rîmaru had killed four women - Mihaela Ursu, Gheorghiţa Popa, Fănica Ilie, Elena Oprea, and attempted to kill another six - Olga Bărăitaru, Elisabeta Florea, Gheorghiţa Sfetcu, Maria Iordache, Margareta Enache, Elena Buluci. The tribunal condemned him for 23 repeated offences, such as robbery, qualified theft, attempted rape, rape, attempted murder with grievous bodily harm, qualified murder and highly aggravated murder. For all these, leaving aside the offence of highly aggravated murder, he received a total of 219 years imprisonment. For the offence of highly aggravated murder he was condemned to death.

He was also made to pay several sums of money, as compensation, to the civil parties involved in the trial. This was an impressive sum for 1971 - 33,167 Lei, to which were added further 6,500 Lei towards the State, for judicial expenses. In total, he had to pay 39,667 Lei. In addition the Court decided to confiscate 1/3 of his possessions.

In the moment the president of the court uttered the sentence, the public applauded again. Unable to believe he had been condemned to death, Rîmaru was overcome by fury. It was only then that he realised it was all over, and he reacted like a man ruled by his instincts: violently.

He didn't get very far because those guarding him noticed

his intentions immediately. His guards were joined by others in plain clothes, until he was surrounded by seven or eight, who pinned him to the ground by his arms, legs and head. In spite of this they were hard put to subdue him, creasing his new penitentiary uniform with their hands. Then they opened his shirt because he claimed he felt bad and was close to fainting after the moments of struggle. In this state he was taken out of the hall. The public, which had initially applauded, seemed now to be also in a state of shock, and they maintained the hubbub as the militiamen left with their wriggling prisoner.

The law allowed him to declare an appeal within 10 days after the pronouncement of the sentence. He did it verbally the same day, beginning his request for an appeal with the words: "The Undersigned…, condemned to death because people say… I killed, request to approve the appeal".

The appeal was heard at the Supreme Tribunal on the 13th of September. There was little to add, the accused had no new evidence to prove his innocence, and the strategy of his lawyer had already been fought successfully in the first court.

Nevertheless, Rîmaru himself tried to transfer the blame partially from his father to an Arab he claimed to have met two years previously. This man, called Ahmed, was the kind who caressed him and who, one night, "ran to me, took my member and sucked it".

According to Rîmaru, Ahmed had often offered him opium cigarettes which produced a hallucinogenic effect and, under their influence, it is possible that he acted in a criminal manner. But, Rîmaru also declared, Ahmed was the one who committed the majority of the murders and rapes, making him participate in some of them. The story was so fantastic that the judges from the Supreme Court did not consider it for one moment.

"I deeply regret, and from my whole conscience, everything I did and in the name of providence I ask you to leave me my life, although I did not do the same for others.

In the light of the legislation of our socialist state, I remain full of hope and wait for the decision you will come to. You will contribute through this, in a humane way, to the life of a man who was not capable of leaving life to other people, but who nevertheless can still be useful in society after serving my punishment.

Mr President, these deeds were committed as a consequence of my soul's disturbance in not finding understanding in the environment I had around me. I ask that I should at least be understood by you who are the law-maker, and grant justice to those who don't have it. I may not be worthy of this but I appeal however to the kindness and clemency of the honourable Supreme Tribunal. I promise that during the years of detention I will be an example of discipline in order to be able to demonstrate that I will rehabilitate myself. I want to live! *Să trăiți!*"(May you have a long life)

(Rîmaru's appeal, 13th of September 1971)

The appeal was rejected in September.
The punishment received by Rîmaru was not considered

too harsh because, in public opinion, a murderer who had shown proof of cannibalism, vampirism and necrophiliac tendencies deserved to die. There was no discussion of the judicial framework, or the decisions made by the Court. On the contrary, it was the general view that the trial was correct, and that all parties involved, judges, prosecutors, the legal defence, showed remarkable professionalism. The death penalty, however, was something unusual, imposed in exceptional cases where it was necessary to give an example to the whole society.

During the Ceaușescu regime, when odious murders were committed or national safety was at stake, the perpetrators could be condemned to heavy years in prison or to death. The Penal Code stipulated the death penalty for offences of this kind, as well as for embezzlement of large sums that damaged the state. There was no rule with regard to the time which had to pass from the moment of sentencing to the execution itself. Sometimes this was organized quickly, in several days, or weeks. At other times, it could be postponed. The issue of political will in this matter was important. In such cases, the question that mattered was simple. How soon did Ceaușescu want the prisoner to die?

Chapter 15

There is no evidence to suggest that Ceauşescu ordered Rîmaru's speedy execution, but it is likely that the authorities responsible for the procedure did not need to be prompted. It was clear that whole affair had to end as soon as possible, and they wanted to show that they could do their job well, and in the shortest possible time.

The death penalty was abolished and replaced by life imprisonment in 1990. Up to that time, executions took place by firing squad, the majority at Jilava prison, several kilometres from Bucharest. Many of those condemned to death escaped execution simply because it was postponed. Most of the files concerning such matters have been destroyed, so there is no way of telling the exact number of executions, but the official record suggests that over the twenty five years of the Ceauşescu regime, there were 104 executions. The rest had their sentences commuted to life imprisonment or long terms in prison.

Jilava was, by tradition, a place where historic massacres and terrible atrocities had taken place. Its cells had seen a list of notorious assassinations, and the prison had an extermination regime which meant that anyone who ended up there would be considered already dead. The oldest part of the complex was called Fort 13, and its ancient cells were the destination of the most serious political opponents of various regimes. Rîmaru was not a political dissident, and his execution didn't do much more than complete the list of famous names who had died there, but it was also a sort of cover for the terrible reputation of the place.

Executions took place in open air, in the grounds to the right of the prison. The space was punctuated by the posts to which the condemned were tied. Decades before, it used to be an orchard of peach trees, and the place had entered collective memory as the Valley of Peach Trees (Valea Piersicilor). Everyone knew what it meant when a prisoner was taken to Valea Piersicilor. No need for explanations, for explicit terms. Valea Piersicilor said it all.

The execution itself was prefaced by a process which was meant to break the prisoner's will, and prepare him for death. A prime example of this process was the legendary "black room". From the time when the date of the execution was set, the prisoner was moved from his cell to a special room, called the black room, and located somewhere near the main entrance to Fort 13, just a few steps away from the main guardroom. There were no windows and, at the moment when the door closed behind the prisoner, a frightening darkness closed in. It was not just an absence of light you could get used to. It was a darkness that was alive, that got into your heart and transformed you, demolished you.

The temperature in the room was maintained at 13 degrees, with a thin layer of cold water on the floor, which climbed up through your feet into your soul. The use of the black room was a successful psychological tactic. Once out of the room, prisoners were completely disorientated. Some had difficulty in recovering their eyesight, and, themselves, asked to be blindfolded. Life had lost its meaning, and the execution that followed was now regarded with joy and expectation. The torture would end. Death would bring freedom. When asked about their last wishes, many prisoners said they wanted to die sooner. The black room had prepared them, and what followed was a mere formality: pulling the trigger.

It is not clear when the regime abandoned the use of the black room, but Rîmaru was subject to new rules and techniques at the time of his execution in 1971. For example, the condemned man's ankles were shackled together and he was handcuffed. A very dangerous prisoner would have, added to the leg shackles, a chain weighing about 10 kilos, and a ball of the same weight which he carried in his arms when moving around.

On top of all this the prisoner was subject to a form of suicide watch. Informer prisoners were selected to keep a constant watch on the condemned man to make sure that he did not devise a method of suicide. At the same time, they had another role. To harass the "living dead man", as they called the condemned one. They swore at him and attacked him physically, repeating that the death penalty was too easy for him, that he was a murderer and should be tortured; that if he weren't executed soon, he would die at their hands anyway, and it would be better to pray God for the day of the execution to come more quickly. They behaved like real monsters, supported by the guards, trying, by this brutal method of psychological pressure, to convince the condemned man that he had no reason to live, thus making it easier for him to accept the execution.

Today there are no records to help us reconstruct the process of Rîmaru's execution. There are, however, witness statements from participants, who described what they thought was the most shocking element, the conduct of the murderer on the point of death. He did not have any last wishes because he struggled ceaselessly. Dragged out of the car which delivered him to the place of execution, he fought, with the energy of a wild beast, until the moment he was tied to the post with his hands behind his back. He tried to rip the clothes off himself with his teeth, and circled round the post to dodge the bullets. During this time, the representative of the tribunal read out loud a short exposition of his crimes. At the end, the commander of the penitentiary received the call to order the execution. Rîmaru continued to struggle. His last words were: "fetch my father, he is the guilty one!" and "I want to live!".

On receiving the order the firing squad delayed for a moment, startled and intimidated by the drama playing out in front of them. Added to this was the fact that Rîmaru kept dodging round the post and was hard to aim at accurately. When they fired the majority of the bullets hit him in the back, but, at last, he was dead.

The pathologist confirmed the death and filled in the death certificate. Rîmaru's body, wrapped in a white sheet and placed in a modest coffin, was buried in the cemetery of the prison situated somewhere at the end of the village, about 5 km away. It was the 23rd of October 1971. In Jilava prison, a place where every stone breathed evil, those present at the event felt that, on that day, they had accomplished a good deed.

Epilogue

After Rîmaru's death, the city was restored to calm. The locals went out onto the streets without anxiety, and the Militia had cut its nocturnal teams and ID checks. Even the regular thieves, who operated mainly at night, felt relieved and returned to their old habits.

Everything seemed to return to normal, even if the street still talked about the Butcher of Bucharest. A few weeks after the execution, gossip had exaggerated the events out of all proportion, and created urban myths that are still in circulation. The rumours, as a rule, referred to the way in which he acted and to the number of his victims. It was believed, for example, that Rîmaru used to drink the blood of his victims, that is why, among the first nicknames he received, was The Vampire of Bucharest. The number of his victims also multiplied every day, turning into many tens or several score.

In addition, although Rîmaru was a young man who felt permanently intimidated by women, stories circulating about him said he was a charming man, loved by girls who went mad for his looks. So much so, that it was girls washing his bloody shirts, thus taking part, indirectly and through secrecy, in his criminal actions. It is interesting that this story so closely resembles the myth of Dracula.

In all these accounts connected to Rîmaru it would have been impossible not to have a rumour in which the Militia or the Securitate had a role. Many of the senior militiamen believed that Florea Rîmaru had been, at the least, an accomplice. As it happened, Florea died the year after his son's execution, by falling off a moving train. Following Rîmaru's original accusations, the story then spread that in 1944 there had been similar killings in Bucharest, in which the only clues left were the shoe print and finger prints of the killer. On examining Florea's body, it seems that his shoe size and fingerprints matched. It was said that the two law enforcement agencies knew this, and in their frustration at being unable to convict him, arranged his accident.

Another story says that Rîmaru is still alive, having been smuggled out of the country by the Securitate. The reason is unclear.

This is how the street functions anywhere in the world. It is true, in this case, that the regime must take part of the blame. The impulse to secrecy, and the lack of information offered to the public, encouraged the Romanians to create fantasies. On the other hand, this process of testing various inventions against the reality, is how a community, where there has been a major and unexplained event, protects itself, learns its lessons and reviews the facts.

The authorities of the city learned more practical lessons. First there were new organising arrangements. The new Rule of Service and Combat of Troops on Guard appeared, which governed the supervision of the Ministry of the Interior to that of the Council for the Security of the State.

After this, things changed again. The centralisation that took place during the Operation Vulturul convinced the regime that there should be a new reform, and that it should centralise all police services.

In April 1972, Decree Nr 130 was elaborated which stipulated the fusion of the Council for the Security of the State and the Ministry of Interior Affairs in a single giant structure, the new Ministry of the Interior. The new institution was composed of the Securitate, the Militia, the Securitate Troops and fire-fighters, the Penitentiaries and the Archives of the State. The decree also mentioned that the Securitate Troops were responsible, if necessary, for maintaining public order and guarding of objectives of special importance.

The Militia made its own reforms. These were timid but urgently necessary. Operation Vulturul highlighted the fact that the Militia was caught on the wrong foot by this case, and it needed reorganisation and new methods of work. So the Computing Centre of the Ministry of the Interior was created in that year. This had the role of automatically interpreting the data of operative interest collected by detectives.

In parallel, analysis, synthesis and operative information were reorganised in special departments for current information to all Militia units. It might also have been the Rîmaru case that determined the Ministry of the Interior to perfect the Militia system which searched the records of the population. From that moment, the information deposited in the archives started to be more efficiently used in the Militia's operational and informational activities. The judicial criminal record was also reintroduced and the system of entries and exits of foreigners from the country was improved.

Several months after the arrest of Rîmaru, the Militia established a new internal structure, the Centre of psychological research and testing, to put a greater accent on instructing the officers in the field of psychology. Furthermore, psychological testing was introduced as an obligatory requirement for Militia recruits, and the role of doctors of psychiatry and psychology became significantly more important in the activity of the officers than it had been until then.

Beyond all these administrative changes generated by the case of the Butcher of Bucharest, Rîmaru's terrible story entered the classrooms of the Militia school, and became a case study taught by professors to the future officers of Militia and Securitate. Rîmaru had now become history.

End

About the Authors

Dr Mike Phillips OBE FRSL, FRSA

Mike Phillips was educated at the University of London (English), the University of Essex (politics), and at Goldsmiths College London (education).

He worked for the BBC as a journalist and broadcaster between 1972 and 1983 before becoming a lecturer in media studies at the University of Westminster. Subsequently, he worked as Cross Cultural Curator at the Tate Galleries in Britain, and then as Acting Director of Arts in Tilburg in the Netherlands.

He was awarded the Arts Foundation Fellowship in 1996 for crime fiction, and the OBE in 2006 for services to broadcasting. He served as a Trustee of the National Heritage Memorial Fund, but he is best known for his crime fiction, including four novels featuring black journalist Sam Dean: **Blood Rights** (1989), which was adapted for BBC television, **The Late Candidate** (1990), winner of the Crime Writers' Association Silver Dagger Award, **Point of Darkness** (1994) and **An Image to Die For** (1995). **The Dancing Face** (1998) is a thriller centred on a priceless Benin mask. **A Shadow of Myself** (2000) is about a black documentary filmmaker working in Prague and a man who claims to be his brother. **The Name You Once Gave Me** (2006) was written as part of a government backed literacy campaign.

Mike Phillips also co-wrote **Windrush: The Irresistible Rise of Multi-Racial Britain** (1998) to accompany a BBC television series telling the story of the Caribbean migrant workers who settled in post-war Britain. **London Crossings: A Biography of Black Britain** (2001), is a series of interlinked essays and stories, a portrait of the city seen from locations as diverse as New York and Nairobi, London and Lodz, Washington and Warsaw. Currently, he writes librettos for the compositions of his music partner Julian Joseph.

Stejărel Olaru

Stejărel Olaru was born on 30 January 1973, graduated from the Faculty of Theology of the University of Bucharest in 2000 and achieved his Masters in Political Sciences at the National School of Political and Administrative Studies, Bucharest. In 2010 he became a Doctor in Military Science and Intelligence, a title conferred by the National Defence University "Carol I", Bucharest.

Between 2001 and 2006 he worked within the Romanian Institute for Recent History, and as a columnist for various newspapers in Romania.

From 2005 to 2010, he was Director General of the Institute for the Investigation of Communist Crimes in Romania. In this capacity, he researched the post-communist judicial system in Romania, and published books on the history, structures, and the activities of the secret service in communist Romania. He also published in the general press and coordinated projects on the most delicate aspects of communism: repression, torture and population control. He was appointed state counsellor to the prime minister of Romania on national security issues in 2006, and Government representative in the National Intelligence Community. In this role he coordinated the Department for National Security Issues, and took part in reforming the legal framework of Romania's national security systems. During his mandate, he visited risk zones such as Iraq, Afghanistan, Kosovo, Bosnia Herzegovina – as well as expert centres in the field of national and international security in the US and UK.

Among his books are **Stasi şi Securitatea** (Stasi and the Securitate - 2005), together with Georg Herbstritt; **Guide to Archives, Research Institutions, Libraries, Societies, Museums and Memorial Places** (2004); **Cei cinci care au speriat Estul** (The Five Who Terrified the East - 2003); **Ziua care nu se uită. 15 noiembrie 1987, Braşov** (The Day We Won't Forget. 15 November 1987, Braşov - 2002) with Marius Oprea; **Securiştii Partidului** (The Party's Securitate Men - 2002). Articles in the national and international press include studies of the former communist secret structures, as well as analyses of the new secret services in Romania.

Stejărel Olaru is presently a university lecturer in the history of Romanian secret services and intelligence gathering.

Index